CONTENTS

WWE *WrestleMania* XXVI Annual

Pedigree

Published 2010
Published by Pedigree Books Limited
Beech Hill House, Walnut Gardens, Exeter, Devon, EX4 4DH
email: books@pedigreegroup.co.uk
web: www.pedigreebooks.com

£7.99

When Stone Cold Steve Austin took on The Rock at *WrestleMania XIX*, it was the third time these two greats battled each other at *WrestleMania*. It was only the first time that The Rock managed to defeat The Rattlesnake but that might have been something to do with Stone Cold having spent the night prior to the match in the hospital.

The first match in *WrestleMania* history was Tito Santana against the Executioner. Tito Santana would compete in the first nine *WrestleMania* events.

WrestleMania II was the first *WrestleMania* which was available on pay-per-view television leading to the advent of that medium and huge success for WWE.

Both Shawn Michaels and the Big Boss Man made their *WrestleMania* debuts at *WrestleMania V.*

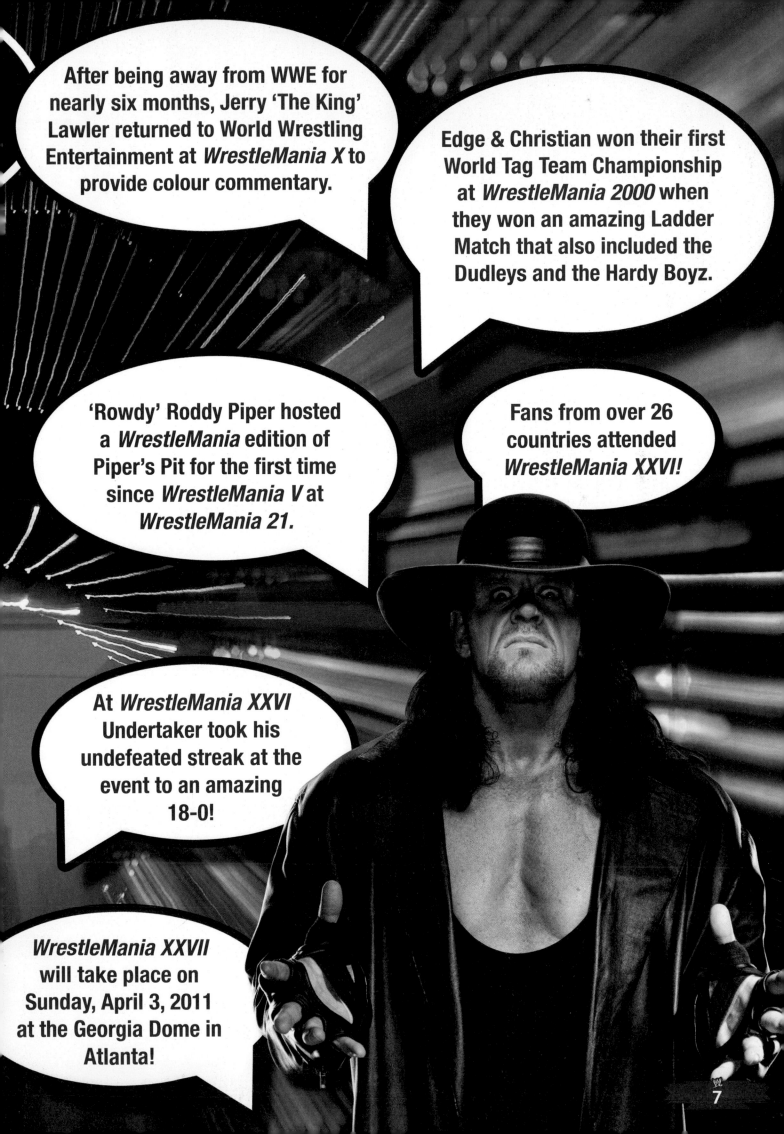

After being away from WWE for nearly six months, Jerry 'The King' Lawler returned to World Wrestling Entertainment at *WrestleMania X* to provide colour commentary.

Edge & Christian won their first World Tag Team Championship at *WrestleMania 2000* when they won an amazing Ladder Match that also included the Dudleys and the Hardy Boyz.

'Rowdy' Roddy Piper hosted a *WrestleMania* edition of Piper's Pit for the first time since *WrestleMania V* at *WrestleMania 21.*

Fans from over 26 countries attended *WrestleMania XXVI!*

At *WrestleMania XXVI* Undertaker took his undefeated streak at the event to an amazing 18-0!

WrestleMania XXVII will take place on Sunday, April 3, 2011 at the Georgia Dome in Atlanta!

RAW

TRIPLE H®

Height:	6-foot-4
Weight:	260 pounds
From:	Greenwich, CT
Signature Move:	Pedigree
Career Highlights:	WWE Champion, World Heavyweight Champion, Undisputed WWE Champion.

Triple H *WrestleMania* Record

March 31, 1996 - *WrestleMania XII:* Ultimate Warrior defeated Hunter Hearst-Helmsley.

March 23, 1997 - *WrestleMania 13:* Hunter Hearst Helmsley w/Chyna defeated Goldust w/Marlena.

March 29, 1998 - *WrestleMania XIV:* Triple H beat Owen Hart to retain the European Championship.

March 28, 1999 - *WrestleMania XV:* Kane beat Triple H by DQ (Chyna turned on Kane and rejoined Triple H and DX).

April 2, 2000 - *WrestleMania 2000:* Triple H defeated The Rock, Mick Foley and Big Show in a Fatal Four Way to retain the WWE Championship.

April 1, 2001 - *WrestleMania X-7:* Undertaker defeated Triple H.

March 17, 2002 - *WrestleMania X8:* Triple H defeated Chris Jericho to become the Undisputed WWE Champion!

March 30, 2003 - *WrestleMania XIX:* Triple H defeated Booker T to retain the World Heavyweight Championship.

March 14, 2004 - *WrestleMania XX:* Chris Benoit beat Triple H and Shawn Michaels to capture the World Heavyweight Championship.

April 3, 2005 - *WrestleMania 21:* Batista defeated Triple H to capture the World Heavyweight Championship.

April 2, 2006 - *WrestleMania 22:* John Cena defeated Triple H to retain the WWE Championship.

March 30, 2008 - *WrestleMania XXIV:* Randy Orton defeated Triple H and John Cena in a Triple Threat Match to retain the WWE Championship.

April 5, 2009- *WrestleMania XXV:* Triple H defeated Randy Orton to retain the WWE Championship.

SHEAMUS™

RAW

Height:	6-foot-6
Weight:	272 pounds
From:	Dublin, Ireland
Signature Move:	Crucifix bomb
Career Highlights:	WWE Champion

Although Sheamus has never competed at *WrestleMania* before, just take a look at his meteoric rise to the top!

June 30, 2009 - ECW on Sci-Fi: **Sheamus (debut) defeated Oliver John.**

October 26, 2009 - *Raw:* **'The Celtic Warrior' Sheamus defeated Jamie Noble.**

November 22, 2009 - *Survivor Series:* **Team Miz defeated Team Morrison in a *Survivor Series* Elimination match (Team Miz consisted of The Miz, Dolph Ziggler, Jack Swagger, Drew McIntyre & Sheamus. Team Morrison consisted of John Morrison, Matt Hardy, Evan Bourne, Shelton Benjamin & Finlay).**

December 13, 2009 - *WWE TLC:* **Sheamus defeated John Cena in a Tables Match to win the WWE Championship.**

December 14, 2009 - Slammy Awards: **Sheamus won the Slammy Award for 2009 "Breakout Superstar of the Year".**

January 31, 2010 - *Royal Rumble:* **Sheamus defeated Randy Orton by DQ to retain the WWE Championship!**

February 21, 2010 - *Elimination Chamber:* **John Cena won the *Raw* Elimination Chamber to win the WWE Championship.**

Sheamus is no stranger to the big stage and with the animosity that has been brewing between these two Superstars, lord only knows what is going to kick off when 'The Irish Curse' is allowed to show what he is made of at the biggest show of the year!

TRIPLE H®

It's the hungry former champion, Sheamus, taking on one of the most decorated competitors of the past 20 years - Triple H!

The Game cost The Celtic Warrior the WWE Championship at Elimination Chamber, and when Sheamus returned on *Raw*, he made sure Triple H felt the brunt of his Irish fury.

Now the two former World Champions face each other at *WrestleMania* to settle a bitter score.

Sheamus has had a meteoric rise since debuting in ECW. When he made the move to *Raw*, he won Jesse Ventura's Breakout Battle Royal to earn a WWE title opportunity against John Cena.

He defeated Cena at WWE TLC: Tables, Ladders and Chairs to be the undisputed Breakout Star of

SHEAMUS™

2009. The Celtic Warrior dominated Monday nights but once he stepped inside the Elimination Chamber, Sheamus was eliminated and then lost the WWE Championship when Triple H pinned him inside Satan's Structure.

This is Sheamus' greatest challenge. The Game is a 13-time World Champion and since making his *WrestleMania* debut in 1996, Triple H has defeated the likes of Chris Jericho, Randy Orton, The Rock and Big Show.

The majority of his *WrestleMania* matches have been main events and so The Cerebral Assassin certainly knows the feeling of headlining on The Grandest Stage of Them All...

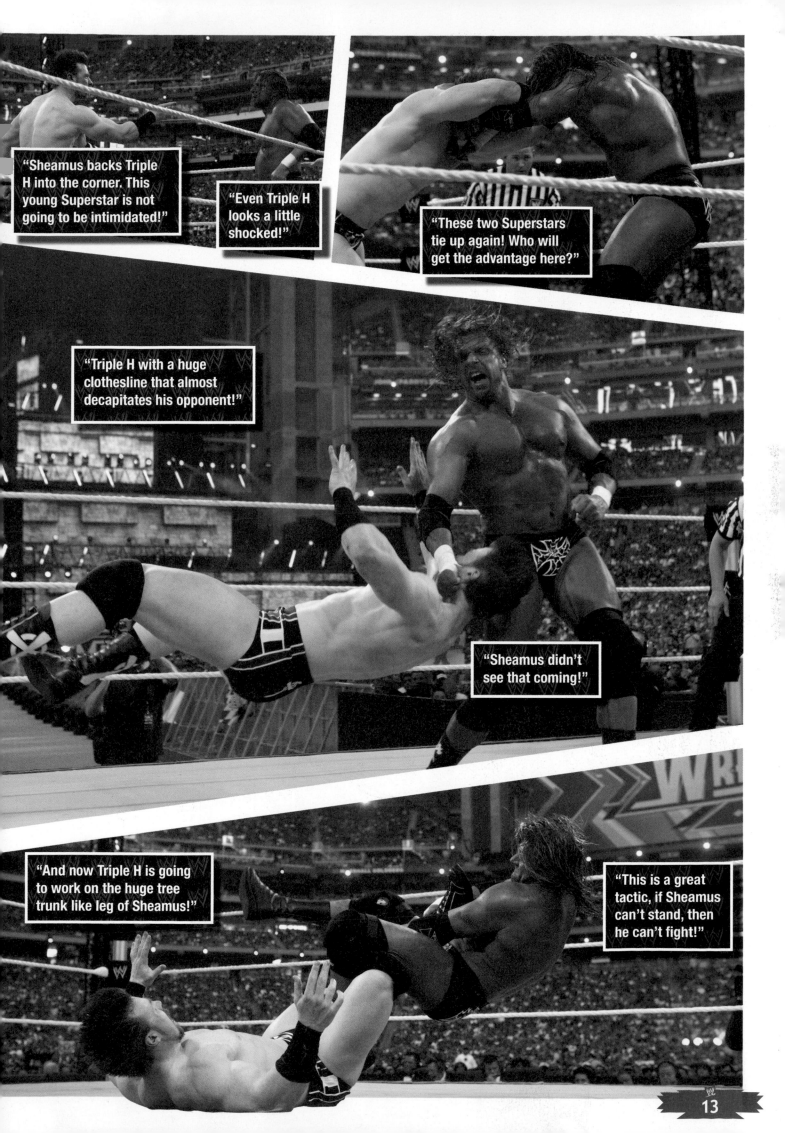

"Sheamus backs Triple H into the corner. This young Superstar is not going to be intimidated!"

"Even Triple H looks a little shocked!"

"These two Superstars tie up again! Who will get the advantage here?"

"Triple H with a huge clothesline that almost decapitates his opponent!"

"Sheamus didn't see that coming!"

"And now Triple H is going to work on the huge tree trunk like leg of Sheamus!"

"This is a great tactic, if Sheamus can't stand, then he can't fight!"

"Would you look at that! Sheamus just sent Triple H crashing into the steel steps!"

"I have felt that before, and believe me, it hurts!"

"Sheamus is pounding away at Triple H's forehead!"

"Sheamus is in complete control here!"

"Sheamus with a huge sideslam to the former champion! I could feel the impact from here!"

"I can not believe how well Sheamus is doing in his *WrestleMania* debut!"

"And he follows it up with huge clothesline!"

"Sheamus is slowing the pace a little here which may be a mistake! Although he is wearing down Triple H with that move!"

"Sheamus is stomping away at Triple H! Things are not looking good for 'The Game'."

"Triple H just can't escape from the corner!"

"This is a great tactic from Sheamus, he has isolated Triple H and cut off the ring!"

"Sheamus with a huge powerslam to Triple H!"

"The whole ring shook from the impact of that move!"

"Sheamus has Triple H set up for the Irish Curse! If he can hit this move it may be all over!"

"But Triple H somehow escaped from that attempt!"

"Triple H escaped the attempted signature move from Sheamus, but receives a huge boot to the face for his trouble!"

"I don't think Sheamus is done with Triple H yet! He wants to inflict more punishment first!"

"This could be a rookie mistake from the Irishman!"

"Sheamus needs to make the pin here!"

"Sheamus whips Triple H into the corner and follows up with a big splash!"

"But look at that! Triple H managed to lift his boot and Sheamus ran face first into his foot!"

"Triple H with a high knee! The momentum of this match might be about to change here!"

"Spinebuster! Spinebuster! Shades of Arn Anderson there! Triple H has regained control of the match!"

"Triple H with a boot to the gut! He could be setting up for the Pedigree!"

"We have seen Triple H do this so many times before!"

"Pedigree! Pedigree! Triple H just hit the Pedigree on Sheamus! Go for the pin Triple H!"

"1...2...3! Triple H has pinned Sheamus!"

"Triple H is victorious once again at *WrestleMania*! What a match!"

"Triple H has proven once again why he is known as 'The Game'."

"Sheamus put up a great fight but experience has prevailed here tonight!"

WRESTLEMANIA®

SO HERE WE ARE ONCE AGAIN, TESTING YOUR KNOWLEDGE OF THE GREATEST EVENT ON THE WWE CALENDAR, *WRESTLEMANIA*. DO YOU HAVE WHAT IT TAKES TO GO ALL THE WAY TO THE MAIN EVENT? LET'S FIND OUT!

Q1 Who defeated Ric Flair to end his career at *WrestleMania XXIV?*

A. Shawn Michaels ☐
B. John Cena ☐
C. Triple H ☐

Q2 Who is this Superstar that remains undefeated at *WrestleMania?*

A. Kane ☐
B. Undertaker ☐
C. Triple H ☐

Q3 Who won the United States Championship at *WrestleMania XX?*

A. John Cena ☐
B. Big Show ☐
C. Edge ☐

Q4 Who defeated 'Superfly' Jimmy Snuka at *WrestleMania VI?*

A. Rick Rude ☐
B. Undertaker ☐
C. Chris Jericho ☐

Q5
Who is this Superstar that competed at the first *WrestleMania*?

A. Tito Santana ☐
B. Junkyard Dog ☐
C. King Kong Bundy ☐

Q6
At which Arena did the inaugural *WrestleMania* take place?

A. MSG ☐
B. Nassau Coliseum ☐
C. Wembley Stadium ☐

Q7
Who did Triple H face in his first *WrestleMania* match?

A. The Rock ☐
B. Goldust ☐
C. Ultimate Warrior ☐

Q8
Who is this Superstar that competed in the first-ever *Money In The Bank Ladder Match*?

A. Edge ☐
B. Christian ☐
C. Chris Jericho ☐

Q9
Who won the World Heavyweight Championship at *WrestleMania 22*?

A. Randy Orton ☐
B. Rey Mysterio ☐
C. Big Show ☐

Q10
Who did Undertaker defeat at *WrestleMania XV*?

A. Big Show ☐
B. Big John Studd ☐
C. Big Bossman ☐

MONEY IN THE BANK LADDER MATCH PROFILES

Name: **Matt Hardy**
Height: **6-foot-2**
Weight: **236 pounds**
From: **Cameron, NC**
Signature Move:
Twist of Fate

Hardy is no stranger to this kind of extreme match. He and his brother re-invented the tag team division in the late 90's and early 2000's with their incredible series of TLC matches against foes such as Edge and Christian. Hardy's never say die attitude will always make him a dangerous competitor in this match!

Name: **Kofi Kingston**
Height: **6-foot-1**
Weight: **200 pounds**
From: **Jamaica**
Signature Move:
Cool Runnings

Kofi Kingston is one of the most gifted athletes in WWE today. His vertical leap means that he has a huge advantage when it comes to climbing the ladder as he can reach half way up in just a single bound. Competing in his second consecutive Money in the Bank Ladder Match, Kofi will be hoping to win.

Name: **Evan Bourne**
Height: **5-foot-9**
Weight: **183 pounds**
From: **St Louis, MO**
Signature Move:
Shooting Star Press

Earning the eighth spot in the match after defeating William Regal on Raw, the always exciting, high-flying Evan Bourne will make his Money in The Bank debut this year. Risk taking Bourne has a great chance at claiming victory. With his Shooting Star Press, other Superstars have to be worried every time he competes!

Name: **Shelton Benjamin**
Height: **6-foot-2**
Weight: **248 pounds**
From: **Orangeburg, SC**
Signature Move:
T-bone Suplex

Shelton Benjamin is perhaps the most experienced participant in the match as this will be his fifth time competing in the Money in The Bank Ladder Match. After coming so close to winning the match on many occasions in the past, Benjamin would have to be considered a favourite!

Name: MVP
Height: 6-foot-3
Weight: 249 pounds
From: Miami, FL
Signature Move:
The Playmaker

Although MVP may not be known as a high-flyer like so many of the other competitors, he is tough as nails and can brawl with the best of them. This will not be the first time MVP has competed in the match and after a great showing at *WrestleMania 25*, he will want to take it one step further this year and grab the briefcase!

Name: Jack Swagger
Height: 6-foot-4
Weight: 263 pounds
From: Perry, OK
Signature Move:
Gutwrench Powerbomb

The 'All-American, American' Jack Swagger will be competing in his first-ever WrestleMania and his first Money in The Bank Ladder Match at *WrestleMania XXVI*. Swagger is certainly not short on confidence but will this most extreme match suit his amateur background?

Name: Christian
Height: 6-foot-2
Weight: 235 pounds
From: Toronto, ON
Signature Move:
The Killswitch

After defeating Carlito on Raw in a hard-fought match, Christian became the first man to qualify for this year's Money in the Bank Ladder Match. Knowing that every Superstar who has won the match in the past has gone on to win a World Championship, Christian must realise that this is a great opportunity for him!

Name: Dolph Ziggler
Height: 6-foot
Weight: 221 pounds
From: Hollywood, FL
Signature Move:
Zig Zag

February 2010, Dolph Ziggler defeated both R-Truth and John Morrison in a match on *SmackDown* to qualify for the Money in the Bank Ladder Match at *WrestleMania*. Without doubt, this young stud will be looking to make an impact and the other Superstars are going to have to watch their backs!

Name: Kane
Height: 7-foot-0
Weight: 323 pounds
From: Parts Unknown
Signature Move:
Chokeslam

At *WrestleMania 25*, Kane competed in the Money in The Bank Ladder Match and came within inches of victory. As Kane reached for the briefcase, CM Punk delivered a brutal martial arts kick to the head of the Big Red Monster sending him crashing to the mat from the top of the ladder.

Name: Drew McIntyre
Height: 6-foot-5
Weight: 18 stone
From: Ayr, Scotland
Signature Move:
Scot Drop

By rights, Drew McIntyre should not even be in the match! The Intercontinental Champion's undefeated streak came to an end when Kane defeated him on *SmackDown*. However, being a favourite of Mr McMahon, he was eventually given a third opportunity at qualifying when he scored a victory.

ARIZON

WRES

·X·

The most fearless and talented competitors will risk everything in a Money in the Bank Ladder Match in a bid to compete for a World Championship.

This year, for the first time since the event began in 2005, an unprecedented ten Superstars will do battle at *WrestleMania XXVI.*

This dangerous contest pits Superstars against each other in a battle to climb a ladder and snatch a briefcase hanging above the ring. The case holds a contract giving the winner an opportunity to face a World Champion over the next 12 months.

This ability to 'cash-in' a championship opportunity has often given Money in the Bank winners a serious advantage over their opponents.

K LADDER MATCH

MANIA VI

Edge, the first-ever 'Mr Money in the Bank,' used his contract at New Year's Revolution 2006 and defeated WWE Champion John Cena immediately after the 12 Rounds star had just successfully defended his title in an Elimination Chamber Match.

At Extreme Rules in 2009, CM Punk faced Jeff Hardy moments after The Charismatic Enigma defeated Edge for the World Heavyweight Championship in a grueling Tables, Ladders and Chairs Match.

Every Superstar who has cashed in a Money in the Bank contract has won a World Championship, including CM Punk, who won the contest at *WrestleMania* in 2008 and 2009.

Which of these ten Superstars will snatch the briefcase and contract...

"This is the match I have been waiting for! The Money in the Bank Ladder Match!"

"And here comes our first competitor, the always exciting Kofi Kingston!"

"And next out to the ring in his second Money in the Bank Match, MVP!"

"MVP has been on a roll of late, he has a great chance in this match!"

"This guy has to be my pick for the match! Evan Bourne!"

"Evan Bourne is not afraid of taking risks, this could be his perfect match!"

The All-American American, Jack Swagger is out next! I am not sure how well suited Swagger will be for this kind of match."

"His amateur background won't be of much use tonight!"

"The fifth competitor in the match is Shelton Benjamin!"

"He has competed in all but one of the Money in the Bank Ladder Matches at *WrestleMania*!"

"No stranger to a ladder match, here comes Matt Hardy!"

"Hardy will be looking to get a World Title opportunity!"

"Perhaps the most devious man in this match is out next, Dolph Ziggler!"

"Ziggler will have to use every trick in the book just to survive in this match!"

"Now this guy should not even be in this match!"

"You're right! The Intercontinental Champion lost his qualifying match against Kane, but being a favourite of Mr McMahon, Drew McIntyre was given another chance!"

"The ninth competitor to enter the match is also the largest competitor in the match, the always dangerous, Kane!"

"And finally, here comes Christian!"

"Christian was actually the first man to qualify for this match and he will be looking to go all the way this year!"

"The match is underway and MVP goes right after the Intercontinental Champion, Drew McIntyre!"

"Evan Bourne uses his speed and agility to climb the ladder!"

"What a huge boot to the face!"

"But he is pulled down by Kane who then knocks Matt Hardy down to the canvas!"

"Kofi Kingston has Kane in the corner and is pounding away at his forehead!"

"Kane might have some bad intentions though!"

"Kane with a powerbomb onto the ladder! That must have broken Kofi in half!"

"This match will certainly shorten your career!"

"Shelton Benjamin is going for the briefcase!"

"But Jack Swagger uses the ladder like a battering ram and knocks Shelton back down to the mat!"

"Jack Swagger is going crazy with that ladder! He just took out MVP!"

"MVP crashes to the outside!"

"Christian and Evan Bourne just knocked Hardy from the top of the ladder!"

"And that was not a pretty landing for Matt Hardy!"

"Kane takes out both Shelton Benjamin and MVP with a ladder shot!"

"You could hear metal hitting skull all over this great arena!"

"Evan Bourne and Matt Hardy are up on the ladder now!"

"Look at that! Matt Hardy just hip tossed Evan Bourne from the top of the ladder!"

"What is Kofi Kingston doing here?"

"He is using a broken ladder as a pair of stilts! Will he be able to reach the briefcase like that?"

"Hardy and Christian are battling back though!"

"Twist of Fate! Twist of Fate from the top of the ladder!"

"A double boot to the face sends Kane flailing from the top of the ladder to the floor below!"

"Both men crash to the canvas! I am not sure who came out worse from that move!"

"But look! Everyone else is down and Jack Swagger has climbed the ladder!"

"Jack Swagger has the briefcase!"

"From out of nowhere, Swagger took his opportunity and climbed the ladder to win the match!"

"Jack Swagger has won the Money in the Bank Ladder Match at *WrestleMania*!"

"He will now get a shot at whichever World Champion he wants to take on! And remember, almost every Superstar who has won this match in the past has gone on to become a World Champion!"

Mania Moment Number 12

Undertaker vs 'Superfly' Jimmy Snuka
WrestleMania VII
March 24, 1991

This was a pinnacle moment in *WrestleMania* history as it marked the beginning of Undertaker's undefeated streak at the event! Undertaker was accompanied to the ring by Paul Bearer and defeated Snuka with a Tombstone Pile Driver! Something he would go on to repeat a further 18 times over the course of his career. Never has a Superstar been more dominating at *WrestleMania* than The Deadman!

Mania Moment Number 11

Money In The Bank Ladder Match
WrestleMania 21
April 3, 2005

WrestleMania 21 marked the first time the Money In The Bank Ladder Match was held at the event - participants would battle it out in the hope of being able to claim a title shot at a later date. The match is perhaps the most innovative creation in WWE history and has produced countless show-stopping moments. Since the first time this match appeared on the card, it has become a favourite with the WWE Universe.

Mania Moment Number 10

Tito Santana vs The Executioner
WrestleMania
March 31, 1985

The match that started it all! The very first match at the very first *WrestleMania*. Although there were no titles on the line in the opening bout, everybody knew that when those curtains opened for the first time, a new era in sports-entertainment had begun. After years of planning in Mr McMahon's mind, his child was born and the future of not only WWE, but also television as a whole, would never be the same again!

Mania Moment Number 9

WWE Championship Tournament Final
Randy 'Macho Man' Savage vs 'Million Dollar Man' Ted DiBiase
WrestleMania IV
March 27, 1988

The first time that the WWE Championship changed hands at a *WrestleMania* event was at *WrestleMania IV* when Randy Savage won the vacant title. The odds were stacked against Savage as in DiBiase's corner were both Virgil, and the legendary Andre the Giant. Savage battled against all three men during the bout and through sheer grit and determination, managed to pull out the win!

Mania Moment Number 8

WWE Championship Match
Bret 'Hit Man' Hart vs Yokozuna
WrestleMania IX
April 4, 1993

For the first time in history, the WWE Championship would change hands twice at *WrestleMania*. Yokozuna, with a little help from Mr Fuji, defeated Bret Hart, only to be challenged by Hulk Hogan immediately after the match. Hogan scored the pin and once again took the glory. It was also the first time a *WrestleMania* had been held outdoors. The event also featured one of the funniest moments in WWE history as Bobby 'The Brain' Heenan arrived at the arena on a camel!

Mania Moment Number 7

Owen Hart vs. Bret 'Hit Man' Hart
WrestleMania X
March 20, 1994

Never before had two brothers faced off at *WrestleMania*. In a match so technically brilliant many believed it was worthy of main event status, Owen defeated his older brother and later in the night Bret went on to defeat Yokozuna to become the new WWE Champion! Since then there have been several Brother vs Brother matches at *Mania* including Jeff vs Matt Hardy and Kane vs Undertaker.

WRESTLEMANIA

SO HERE WE ARE AT THE SECOND PART OF OUR *WRESTLEMANIA* QUIZ. HOW ARE YOU DOING SO FAR? REMEMBER TO KEEP NOTE OF YOUR SCORE!

Q1 Who won the Diva Battle Royal at *WrestleMania 25*?

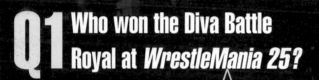

A. Beth Phoenix ☐
B. Michelle McCool ☐
C. Santina Marella ☐

Q2 Who is this Superstar that fought in the opening bout of *WrestleMania XXIV*?

A. Hornswoggle ☐
B. MVP ☐
C. Finlay ☐

Q3 Who did Undertaker defeat to become the World Heavyweight Champion for the first time?

A. Triple H ☐
B. Batista ☐
C. Edge ☐

Q4 Who sang America the Beautiful at *WrestleMania 23*?

A. POD ☐
B. Aretha Franklin ☐
C. Lilian Garcia ☐

QUIZ PART TWO

Q5
Who is this Superstar that Andre the Giant defeated at the first *WrestleMania*?

A. King Kong Bundy ☐
B. The Mountie ☐
C. Big John Studd ☐

Q6
Who defeated Mr McMahon at *WrestleMania X-Seven*?

A. Stone Cold Steve Austin ☐
B. Shane McMahon ☐
C. Undertaker ☐

Q7
Who is The Ringmaster better known as?

A. Stone Cold Steve Austin ☐
B. Vader ☐
C. The Rock ☐

Q8
At which *WrestleMania* did Shawn Michaels and Razor Ramon compete in a Ladder Match?

A. *WrestleMania X* ☐
B. *WrestleMania IX* ☐
C. *WrestleMania XI* ☐

Q9
Who is this Superstar that competed at *WrestleMania X-Seven* in the Gimmick *Battle Royal*?

A. The Goon ☐
B. The Iron Sheik ☐
C. Tugboat ☐

Q10
Who did Ricky 'The Dragon' Steamboat defeat in his *WrestleMania* debut?

A. Matt Bourne ☐
B. Hercules Hernandez ☐
C. Greg Valentine ☐

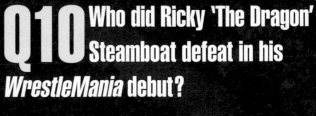

WRESTLEMANIA CROSSWORD

USE ALL OF YOUR KNOWLEDGE OF *WRESTLEMANIA'S* PAST AND PRESENT TO WORK OUT THE CLUES AND FILL IN THE ANSWERS!

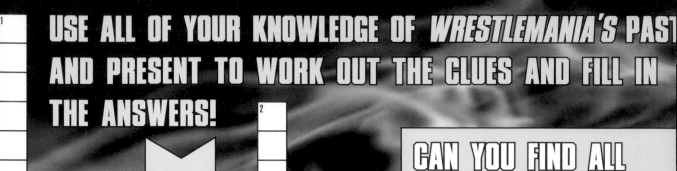

CAN YOU FIND ALL TEN OF THE MONEY IN THE BANK LADDER MATCH PARTICIPANTS HIDDEN WITHIN THIS WORDSEARCH?

Across answers filled in: 3. BMBURN, 4. KANE (down), 5. UNDERTAKER (down), 7. EDGE, 10. KOFI KINGSTON, 6. SHAWN MICHAELS (down)

ACROSS

3. He won *The Money in The Bank Ladder Match* twice!
7. The Rated R Superstar.
8. She is Miss *WrestleMania*.
10. He used a broken ladder as a pair of stilts!

DOWN

1. He made his *WrestleMania* return at *WrestleMania XXVI*.
2. He faced Triple H at *WrestleMania 25*.
4. The Big Red Monster.
5. Still undefeated.
6. He was retired at *WrestleMania XXVI*.
9. He defeated Big Show in a Sumo Match!

WRESTLEMANIA® WORDSEARCH

N	U	K	T	T	Q	O	S	E	C	X	R	K	D	D	K	W	E	X	N	W	R
O	I	T	O	C	D	S	U	H	E	E	Q	C	Y	Y	U	O	M	C	O	I	D
J	T	M	T	Y	T	M	R	C	L	Q	W	U	S	O	B	E	N	T	T	V	I
W	Q	U	A	V	G	I	T	G	U	Y	V	O	B	F	X	V	U	A	S	W	Z
Z	N	I	P	J	S	F	G	W	Y	D	R	A	H	T	T	A	M	J	G	T	G
K	X	O	Q	T	N	I	C	S	Z	H	Q	U	Y	H	K	N	K	P	N	X	G
H	Z	S	I	U	Z	E	W	Y	I	J	W	Y	X	B	F	B	S	M	I	W	J
T	Z	A	S	H	Z	N	B	D	D	F	A	W	J	U	J	O	C	X	K	U	Y
Z	N	M	P	P	X	D	F	N	X	W	V	C	N	D	C	U	R	O	I	O	I
V	W	L	O	X	N	Z	E	J	O	K	S	V	K	B	U	R	L	H	F	D	N
P	O	D	R	E	W	M	C	I	N	T	Y	R	E	S	A	N	S	N	O	N	S
D	K	I	Q	Y	Y	B	S	I	E	L	L	K	R	G	W	E	M	D	K	M	A
E	R	E	W	X	H	W	K	Q	H	K	M	E	R	U	M	A	U	L	R	K	C
E	N	P	O	H	W	X	U	P	K	E	H	B	H	C	Y	V	G	M	I	I	U
E	L	A	M	C	M	E	R	T	D	U	F	A	B	S	D	C	U	G	K	G	K
D	V	V	K	L	C	Z	N	M	W	E	R	T	Y	Q	K	K	W	P	E	P	Z
Z	V	L	D	O	K	G	J	Z	T	H	I	P	Z	W	A	F	F	D	Q	R	L
N	L	H	X	W	L	I	V	J	J	M	W	W	H	U	F	P	Z	E	X	I	V
W	I	M	Z	R	H	U	X	P	T	Z	Y	U	J	U	M	O	E	H	X	A	A
H	F	K	D	G	R	G	C	E	U	J	N	Y	O	F	Z	V	R	S	W	E	R
R	E	T	R	O	P	S	U	O	I	V	A	T	N	O	V	L	E	T	N	O	M
Y	A	O	K	J	Z	X	P	H	D	D	C	I	N	V	T	L	H	I	D	B	I

CHRISTIAN	**KANE**
DOLPH ZIGGLER	**KOFI KINGSTON**
DREW McINTYRE	**MATT HARDY**
EVAN BOURNE	**MONTEL VONTAVIOUS PORTER**
JACK SWAGGER	**SHELTON BENJAMIN**

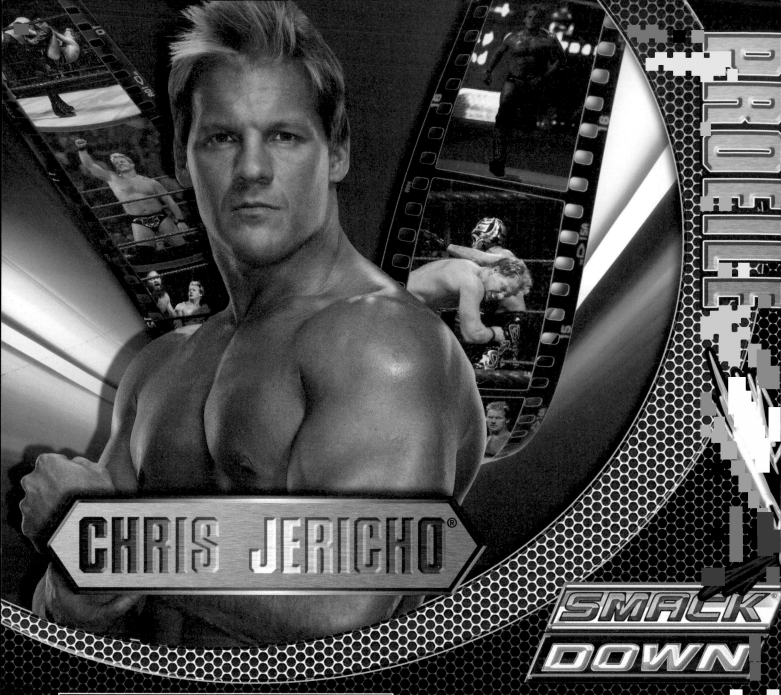

CHRIS JERICHO

SMACK DOWN

Height:	6-foot
Weight:	226 pounds
From:	Manhasset, NY
Signature Move:	Codebreaker, Walls of Jericho
Career Highlights:	Undisputed WWE Champion, World Heavyweight Champion

Chris Jericho's *WrestleMania* Record

April 2, 2000 - *WrestleMania 2000:* Chris Jericho won the European Championship.

April 1, 2001 - *WrestleMania X-7:* Chris Jericho defeated William Regal to retain the Intercontinental Championship.

March 17, 2002 - *WrestleMania X8:* Triple H defeated Chris Jericho for the Undisputed WWE Championship.

March 30, 2003 - *WrestleMania XIX:* Shawn Michaels defeated Chris Jericho.

March 14, 2004 - *WrestleMania XX:* Christian defeated Chris Jericho.

April 3, 2005 - *WrestleMania 21:* Chris Jericho competed in the Money in the Bank Ladder Match.

March 30, 2008 - *WrestleMania XXIV:* Chris Jericho competed in the Money in the Bank Ladder Match.

April 5, 2009 - *WrestleMania 25:* Chris Jericho defeated Legends 'Superfly' Jimmy Snuka, Ricky 'The Dragon' Steamboat & Rowdy Roddy Piper w/Ric Flair.

March 28, 2010 - *WrestleMania XXVI:* Chris Jericho defeated Edge to retain the World Heavyweight Championship.

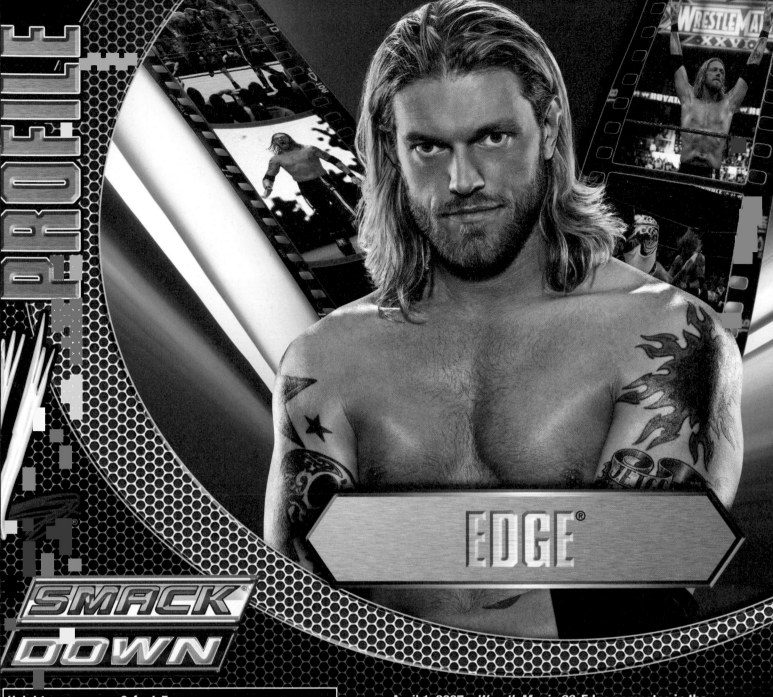

SMACK DOWN

EDGE

Height:	6-foot-5
Weight:	250 pounds
From:	Toronto, ON
Signature Move:	Spear
Career Highlights:	WWE Champion, World Heavyweight Champion

Edge's WrestleMania Record

April 2, 2000 – *WrestleMania 2000:* Edge & Christian defeated The Hardy Boyz & The Dudley Boyz.

April 1, 2001 - *WrestleMania X-7:* Edge & Christian beat The Dudley Boyz & The Hardy Boyz in "TLC 2" to win the Tag titles!

March 17, 2002 - *WrestleMania X8:* Edge defeats Booker T.

April 3, 2005 - *WrestleMania 21:* Edge wins the Money In The Bank Ladder Match.

April 2, 2006 - *WrestleMania 22:* Edge w/Lita defeated Mick Foley in a Hardcore Match.

April 1, 2007 - *WrestleMania 23:* Edge competes in the Money In The Bank Ladder Match.

March 30, 2008 - *WrestleMania XXIV:* Undertaker defeated Edge.

April 5, 2009 - *WrestleMania 25:* John Cena defeated Edge and Big Show in a Triple Threat Match to win the World Heavyweight Championship.

March 28, 2010 - *WrestleMania XXVI:* Chris Jericho defeated Edge to retain the World Heavyweight Championship.

CHRIS JERICHO

WRES
ARIZON
X

Chris Jericho and Edge used to be inseparable tag team champions and big buddies – before The Rated-R Superstar suffered a torn Achilles tendon last summer and spent seven months recuperating.

Rather than stand by his friend, Jericho turned on Edge. The arrogant superstar claimed that he was responsible for all the successes they enjoyed. The Rated-R Superstar was furious and longed to get his own back on his so-called friend.

Edge will get his chance on The Grandest Stage of Them All when he challenges Jericho for the World Heavyweight Championship at *WrestleMania*.

The Ultimate Opportunist's road to *WrestleMania* began at the *Royal Rumble* when he shocked the WWE Universe by outlasting 29 opponents. The victory allowed him to choose which World title he would aim for.

Jericho's route wasn't so clear. He collided inside the Elimination

MANIA

EDGE®

Chamber with five others, including then-World Heavyweight Champ The Undertaker. As The Deadman appeared set to block Jericho's path to Phoenix, Shawn Michaels superkicked The Phenom, allowing Jericho to win the title and a guaranteed match at *WrestleMania*.

Edge decided to use his *Royal Rumble* conquest to challenge the six-time World Champion. The Rated-R Superstar attacked his outspoken adversary on both *SmackDown* and

Monday Night *Raw*, hitting Jericho with Spear after dangerous Spear at every turn. Jericho blasted his No. 1 Contender with the World Title during the "Highlight Reel."

Jericho followed up with an earth-shattering Codebreaker to his challenger during "The Cutting Edge" on *SmackDown*.

The clash between these former friends is deadly serious. There's no greater enemy than a wronged best friend…

"Jericho comes back with a side suplex!"

"But Edge has recovered and is going for an early pin with a sunset flip!"

"Edge landed right on his surgically repaired neck! That was a great move from Y2J!"

"Jericho just manages to kick out at two!"

"We know what Edge is looking for here! The entire WWE universe is shouting "Spear!""

"Edge is looking to spear Jericho out of his boots!"

"Edge with another flying shoulder block! Edge's ankle seems to have recovered very well!"

"You are right, he is showing no signs of the injury that kept him out of action for half a year!"

"Edge goes for the Spear but Jericho ducks out of the way!"

"But look at that! Edge caught Jericho with a huge boot to the face!"

"Jericho has momentarily taken control with a reverse chin lock!"

"This move is designed to wear your opponent down and sap his energy."

"But Edge has regained his vertical base and takes Jericho over the top rope with a huge clothesline!"

"Edge is all over the champion!"

"Edge has climbed to the top rope and is looking for another high-risk manoeuvre!"

"Edge flies from the ring apron and hits Jericho with a flying clothesline!"

"Jericho is up there to meet him though and both Superstars are fighting it out in a very precarious position."

"Edge loves to take huge risks! I just hope that one pays off!"

"Wow! Edge just hit Jericho with a face buster suplex from the top rope!"

"Edge has gone back to the top and hits a flying cross body block to Chris Jericho!"

"What an incredible move! What an incredible match!"

"But Jericho rolls through and has Edge pinned! 1...2! Edge kicks out!"

"Jericho is going for the Walls of Jericho! Can he turn Edge over?"

"This is going to put some real pressure on Edge's ankle!"

"Edge somehow manages to make it to the ropes, but you can see that the Walls Of Jericho have taken its effect!"

"Jericho has it locked in! Look at the pain etched on Edge's face!"

"Will Edge be forced to tap out here?"

"Jericho with a kick to the back of Edge's head. Edge may be knocked out!"

"Edge with a DDT out of nowhere! That move was just pure instinct!"

"Jericho slowly climbs to the top rope and delivers a huge forearm to the back of Jericho's head!"

"You are right about that! Both men are down! Whoever gets up first will have the advantage in this match!"

"Edge is looking wobbly here! The lights are on but nobody is home!"

"Jericho with a Codebreaker! Codebreaker! Jericho can hit that move so quickly!"

"Edge may have been out on his feet and that gave Jericho the opportunity to hit his signature move!"

"Jericho is going for the pin! 1...2...3! Jericho has retained his title!"

"Edge looked so good in the early stages of this match, but perhaps a little ring rust cost him the match!"

"The look of relief on Jericho's face is evident! He knows how close he came to losing the match!"

"But once again, Jericho has pulled it out of the bag!"

"But wait! While Jericho celebrates on the announce table, Edge has got back to his feet!"

"Spear, Spear, Spear! Edge just speared Jericho through the crowd barrier! Edge has completely lost it!"

"Check out the look on Edge's face! He looks psychotic!"

"There is no doubt that Edge is not happy, and I am sure this rivalry is not over!"

"Although Edge may have lost the match tonight, it is 'The Rated R Superstar' who is standing victorious at the bitter end!"

"I can't wait to see how this situation develops over the following weeks!"

Take a look at these two images from the Money in the Bank Ladder Match at *WrestleMania XXVI*. They both look the same don't they? They aren't! We have made ten small changes can you spot them all?

TEST YOUR KNOWLEDGE ON SOME OF THE GREAT LEGENDS WHO HAVE BEEN INDUCTED INTO THE WWE HALL OF FAME. THESE MEN AND WOMEN MADE THE SPORT THE PHENOMENON THAT IT IS TODAY, SO LET'S SEE WHAT YOU KNOW!

Q1 Who is this Superstar that was the first person to be inducted into The Hall Of Fame?

A. King Kong Bundy
B. George Steel
C. Andre The Giant

Q2 Who was known for entering the ring wearing a chain attached to a dog collar?

A. JYD
B. Y2J
C. MIA

Q3 Who is the son of 'The American Dream'?

A. Cody Rhodes
B. Ted DiBiase
C. Randy Orton

Q4 Who is this Hall Of Famer?

A. The Rock
B. Stone Cold Steve Austin
C. Tito Santana

FAME QUIZ

Q5 In what year was Ricky Steamboat inducted to the Hall of Fame?

A. 2009 ☐
B. 2008 ☐
C. 2007 ☐

Q6 Which Hall of Fame family was known as the first family of World Class Championship Wrestling?

A. The Funks ☐
B. The Heenan Family ☐
C. The Von Erichs ☐

Q7 Who was the last Superstar that Mr Fuji managed in WWE?

A. Ernie Ladd ☐
B. Vader ☐
C. Yokozuna ☐

Q8 What sport is Hall of Famer William Perry more famous for?

A. Baseball ☐
B. American Football ☐
C. Golf ☐

Q9 Who is this Hall of Fame inductee?

A. Jimmy Hart ☐
B. Bob Orton Jr ☐
C. Curt Hennig ☐

Q10 As of *WrestleMania XXVI*, how many Superstars are WWE Hall Of Fame members?

A. 30 ☐
B. 69 ☐
C. 79 ☐

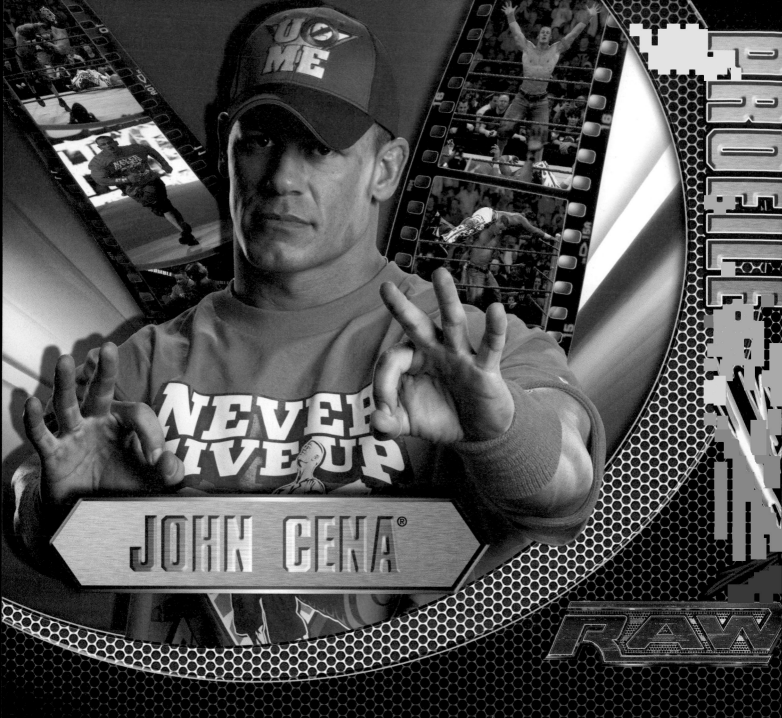

JOHN CENA

Height:	6-foot-1
Weight:	240 pounds
From:	West Newbury, MA
Signature Move:	Attitude Adjustment, STF
Career Highlights:	WWE Champion, World Heavyweight Champion

John Cena's *WrestleMania* Record.

March 14, 2004 – *WrestleMania XX:* John Cena defeats Big Show for the United States Championship.

April 3, 2005 – *WrestleMania 21:* John Cena defeats JBL to win the WWE Championship.

April 2, 2006 – *WrestleMania 22:* John Cena defeats Triple H to retain the WWE Championship.

April 1, 2007 – *WrestleMania 23:* John Cena defeats Shawn Michaels to retain the WWE Championship.

March 30, 2008 – *WrestleMania XXIV:* Randy Orton defeats John Cena and Triple H to retain the WWE Championship.

April 5, 2009 – *WrestleMania 25:* John Cena defeats Big Show and Edge to win the World Heavyweight Championship.

March 28, 2010 – *WrestleMania XXVI:* John Cena defeated Batista to win the WWE Championship.

BATISTA

RAW

Height:	6-foot-6
Weight:	290 pounds
From:	Washington, DC
Signature Move:	Batista Bomb
Career Highlights:	WWE Champion, World Heavyweight Champion

Batista's *WrestleMania* Record.

March 14, 2004 - *WrestleMania XX:* Evolution (Randy Orton/Batista/Ric Flair) beat Mick Foley & The Rock

April 3, 2005 - *WrestleMania 21:* Batista defeated Triple H to capture the World Heavyweight Championship.

April 1, 2007 - *WrestleMania 23:* Undertaker defeated Batista to capture the World Heavyweight Championship.

March 30, 2008 - *WrestleMania XXIV:* Batista (SmackDown) defeated Umaga (Raw) in a Battle for Brand Supremacy.

March 28, 2010--*WrestleMania XXVI:* John Cena defeated Batista to win the WWE Championship.

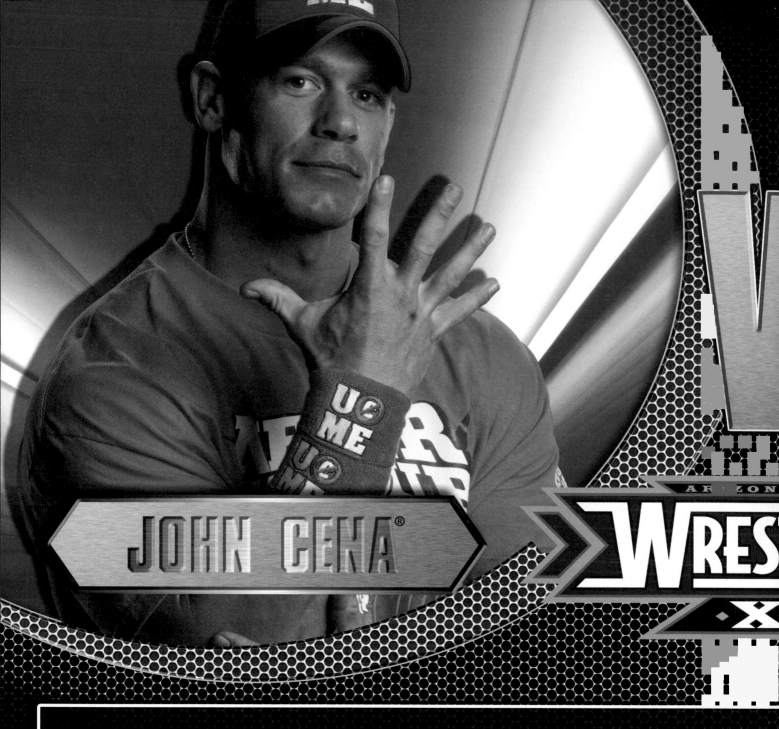

JOHN CENA

There's no love lost between John Cena and Batista. The Animal is insistent that he has the measure of the World Champion – and proved it by taking Cena's WWE Championship.

Cena had just regained his title in an *Elimination Chamber* match against Triple H – but Mr McMahon decreed that he then must immediately fight Batista.

The post-Chamber title match against the Champ saw Batista crush Cena with a vicious Batista Bomb.

But these two giants of WWE are no strangers to each other and have a lot of previous history. In 2005's *Royal Rumble* Cena was one fight from victory before Batista upended him.

WRESTLEMANIA VI · 3·28·2010

BATISTA

He was a whisker away from glory at 2008's *SummerSlam* but The Animal was there again. Cena battled past five other fighters to capture the WWE Title at the *Elimination Chamber* – but Batista took it away.

Almost at every corner, John Cena has found Batista ready to block his path. They were involved in a bitter war of words leading up to

their clash at *WrestleMania XXVI*.

Both men respect each other immensely but there can only be one winner. And both of them believed they would be the victor.

What would happen in this massive rematch? Could Cena get revenge and recapture the WWE Championship? Or would The Animal destroy the former champion?

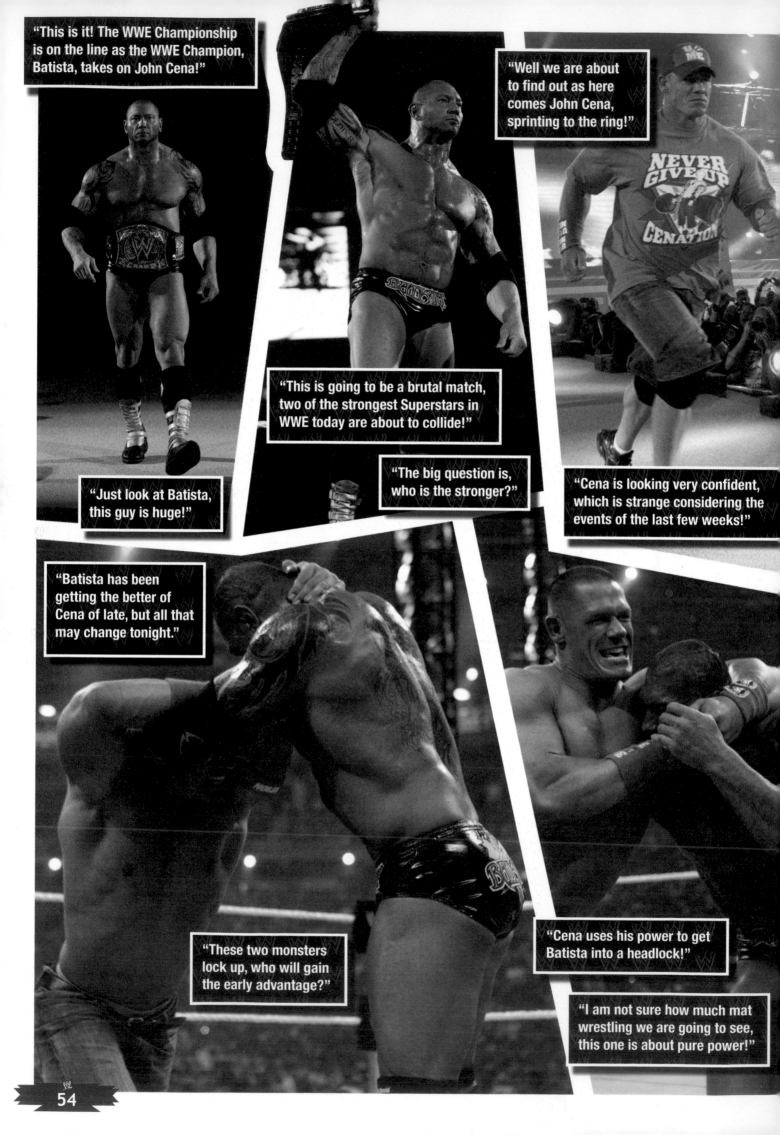

"This is it! The WWE Championship is on the line as the WWE Champion, Batista, takes on John Cena!"

"Well we are about to find out as here comes John Cena, sprinting to the ring!"

"This is going to be a brutal match, two of the strongest Superstars in WWE today are about to collide!"

"Just look at Batista, this guy is huge!"

"The big question is, who is the stronger?"

"Cena is looking very confident, which is strange considering the events of the last few weeks!"

"Batista has been getting the better of Cena of late, but all that may change tonight."

"These two monsters lock up, who will gain the early advantage?"

"Cena uses his power to get Batista into a headlock!"

"I am not sure how much mat wrestling we are going to see, this one is about pure power!"

"Batista with a shoulder block! That was like two trucks colliding!"

"Batista picks up John Cena and rams him into the corner!"

"Batista certainly got the better of John Cena in that exchange!"

"I cannot remember ever seeing Cena out-muscled like this before!"

"Batista with a clubbing blow to the back of John Cena! Batista is being so aggressive in this match thus far!"

"Batista with a boot to the gut! He may be looking for a Batista Bomb early on in the match!"

"But John Cena escapes! That was lucky, the match could have been over!"

"Cena really needs to mount some offence, and quickly!"

"John Cena is in the corner, and here comes Batista looking for a clothesline!"

"Cena just manages to get his boot up and catches Batista square in the face!"

"Cena with a Flying Shoulder Block! Look at the height he got with that move!"

"Cena follows it up with another! John Cena is getting fired up here!"

"The Cenation is right behind him!"

"But Batista is right back up!"

"And the Cenation all know what is about to happen here!"

"You Can't See Me! Cena runs the ropes and drops his fist down onto the face of the champion!"

"Batista is down and Cena may be looking for one of his patented moves!"

"But no! Batista rolled out of the way!"

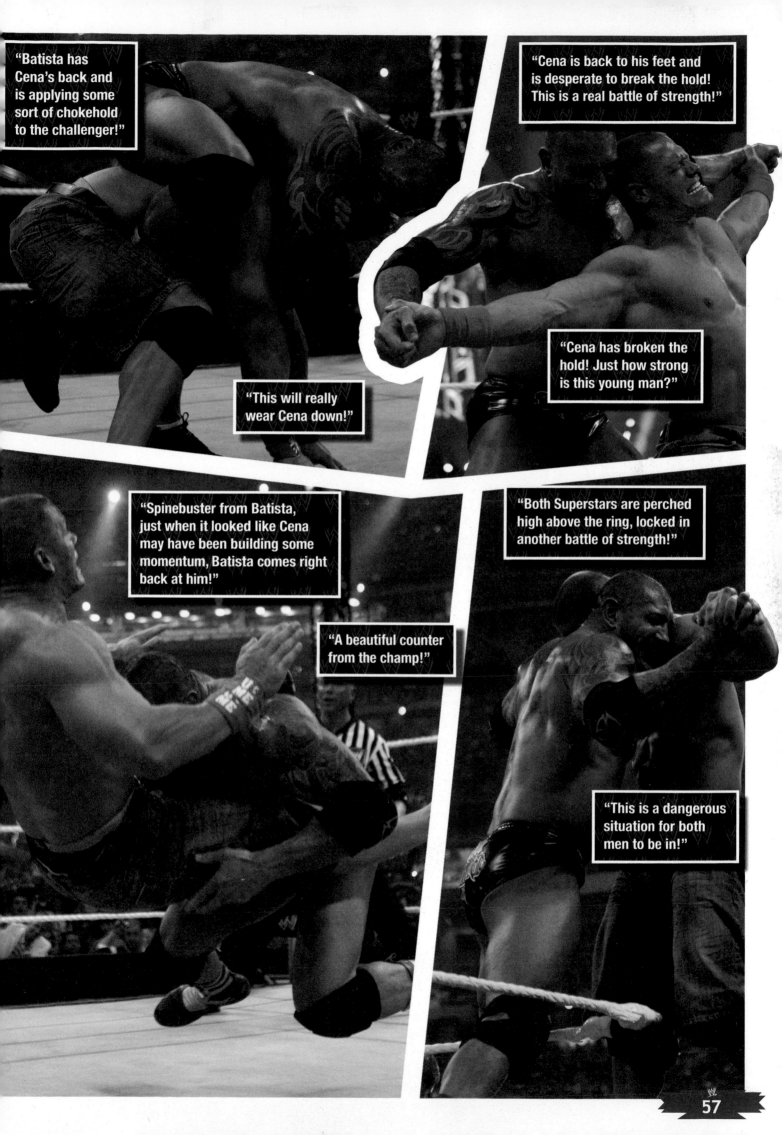

"Batista has Cena's back and is applying some sort of chokehold to the challenger!"

"Cena is back to his feet and is desperate to break the hold! This is a real battle of strength!"

"This will really wear Cena down!"

"Cena has broken the hold! Just how strong is this young man?"

"Spinebuster from Batista, just when it looked like Cena may have been building some momentum, Batista comes right back at him!"

"Both Superstars are perched high above the ring, locked in another battle of strength!"

"A beautiful counter from the champ!"

"This is a dangerous situation for both men to be in!"

"Cena knocks Batista down to the mat from the top rope! What does Cena have in mind here?"

"Cena may be about to go high risk!"

"Five Knuckle Shuffle from the top rope! I have never seen that before!"

"Both Superstars are pulling moves out of the bag tonight! Neither man wants to lose this match!"

"But wait, Cena may have given Batista too long to recover! Batista Bomb!"

"Batista can not believe it! What does he have to do to put Cena away?"

"The match must be over! 1...2...Wow! Cena kicks out of the Batista Bomb, but just barely!"

"Batista knows exactly what to do. He is going for another Batista Bomb!"

"But Cena is countering. He may be looking for a sunset flip here."

"No, look! He has rolled through and grabbed Batista's ankle!"

"Cena may be looking for the STF! Can he lock it in?"

"Cena desperately trying to lock up the giant legs of Batista. But is Batista too near the ropes?"

"Cena has Batista caught in the STF! The referee is asking Batista if he wants to quit."

"Batista just tapped! John Cena has defeated the WWE Champion!"

"What an incredible match. We have a new WWE Champion!"

"John Cena has done it. Against all the odds he has defeated Batista and regained the WWE Championship!

WRESTLEMANIA

HERE'S PART THREE OF THE *WRESTLEMANIA* QUIZ AND THE QUESTIONS IN THIS ROUND ARE ALL ABOUT HOW WELL YOU KNOW THE SUPERSTARS' WRESTLING GEAR! CAN YOU IDENTIFY EACH OF THE TEN SUPERSTARS BELOW FROM JUST LOOKING AT THEIR RING ATTIRE?

Q1
Write here who you think this is...
undertaker

Q2
Write here who you think this is...
John cena

Q3
Write here who you think this is...
finlay

Q4
Write here who you think this is...
John morrison

Q5
Write here who you think this is... *Koffi kingston*

Q6
Write here who you think this is... *EDGE*

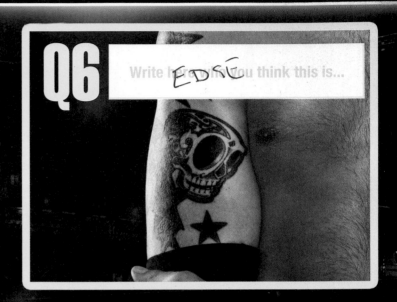

Q7
Write here who you think this is... *Big show*

Q8
Write here who you think this is... *Rey Mysterio*

Q9
Write here who you think this is... *matt hardy*

Q10
Write here who you think this is... *William Regan*

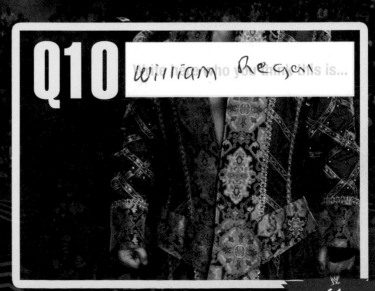

Mania Moment Number 6
Ultimate Warrior vs Hulk Hogan
WrestleMania VI
April 1, 1990

For the first time in the history of *WrestleMania*, the main event would feature a title-for-title match as the Intercontinental Champion, Ultimate Warrior, would take on the WWE Champion, Hulk Hogan. The two Superstars battled it out in front of more than 67,000 fans until Ultimate Warrior secured the victory.

Mania Moment Number 5
Kane vs Chavo Guerrero
WrestleMania XXIV
March 30, 2008

Before *WrestleMania XXIV* went on air, Kane had won a Battle Royal to earn a shot at then ECW Champion, Chavo Guerrero. This would be the first time an ECW Championship had been contested at *WrestleMania* and only the second time an ECW match had taken place at the event. Kane destroyed Chavo Guerrero in just nine seconds, making it the quickest *WrestleMania* match ever!

Mania Moment Number 4
Ric Flair vs Shawn Michaels
WrestleMania XXIV
March 30, 2008

In the most emotionally charged match of the evening, The Heartbreak Kid defeated The Nature Boy thus ending Ric Flair's career. Although both Superstars were great friends outside of the ring, they left nothing in the locker room that night. The match ended when HBK mouthed the words "I'm sorry, I love you!" before delivering Sweet Chin Music to his boyhood hero.

Mania Moment Number 3
Undertaker vs Shawn Michaels
WrestleMania XXVI
March 28, 2010

In another match involving Shawn Michaels, eerily similar to the situation he had found himself in just two years before, HBK was now battling for his own career, this time against Undertaker. On the line was Undertaker's undefeated streak, only on this occasion it would be HBK waving goodbye to the fans when the dust had settled.

Mania Moment Number 2
Bret 'Hit Man' Hart vs Stone Cold Steve Austin
WrestleMania 13
March 23, 1997

At this event, Bret Hart was competing in his 12th consecutive *WrestleMania*. Stone Cold and The Hit Man battled it out in a Submission Match with the World's Most Dangerous Man, Ken Shamrock, acting as referee. In a match that tore the house down, Stone Cold cemented his place as one of the top performers of that era.

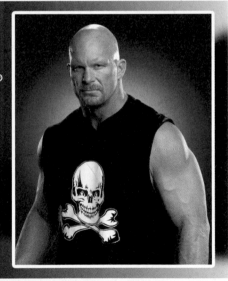

Mania Moment Number 1
Andre The Giant vs Hulk Hogan
WrestleMania III
March 29, 1987

In front of the largest crowd to ever attend a WWE event at the Pontiac Silverdome, Andre The Giant gained his first-ever opportunity at the WWE Championship. With 93,173 fans in attendance, Andre clashed with Hogan at *WrestleMania III* in the biggest match of all time. The Hulkster was victorious, ending the lengthy undefeated streak of his former best friend.

BRET HART®

Height:	6-foot-0
Weight:	234 pounds
From:	Calgary, AB
Signature Move:	The Sharpshooter
Career Highlights:	WWE Champion

Bret Hart's *WrestleMania* Record.

April 2, 1986 - *WrestleMania II:* Bret Hart was the last person eliminated in a 20-man Battle Royal.

March 27, 1987 - *WrestleMania III:* The Hart Foundation and Danny Davis defeated The British Bulldogs and Tito Santana.

March 27, 1988 - *WrestleMania IV:* Bret Hart was the last Superstar eliminated by Bad News Brown in a Battle Royal.

April 2, 1989 - *WrestleMania V:* The Hart Foundation defeated the Honky Tonk Man and Greg Valentine.

April 1, 1990 - *WrestleMania VI:* The Hart Foundation defeated the Bolshivics in just 19 seconds.

March 24, 1991 - *WrestleMania VII:* The Nasty Boys defeated The Hart Foundation.

April 5, 1992 - *WrestleMania VIII:* Bret 'Hit Man' Hart defeated Roddy Piper to recapture the Intercontinental Championship in a classic match.

April 4, 1993 - *WrestleMania IX:* Yokozuna defeated Bret 'Hit Man' Hart to capture the WWE Championship.

March 20, 1994 - *WrestleMania X:* Owen Hart pulled an upset victory over his brother Bret 'Hit Man' Hart in opening match!

April 2, 1995 - *WrestleMania XI:* Bret 'Hit Man' Hart defeated Bob Backlund in a hard-fought 'I Quit' Match.

March 31, 1996 - *WrestleMania XII:* Shawn Michaels defeated Bret 'Hit Man' Hart in an 'Iron Man' match to win the WWE Championship.

March 23, 1997 - *WrestleMania 13:* Bret 'Hit Man' Hart defeated Stone Cold Steve Austin in a Submission Match.

March 28, 2010 – *WrestleMania XXVI:* Bret 'Hit Man' Hart defeated Mr McMahon in a No Holds Barred Match.

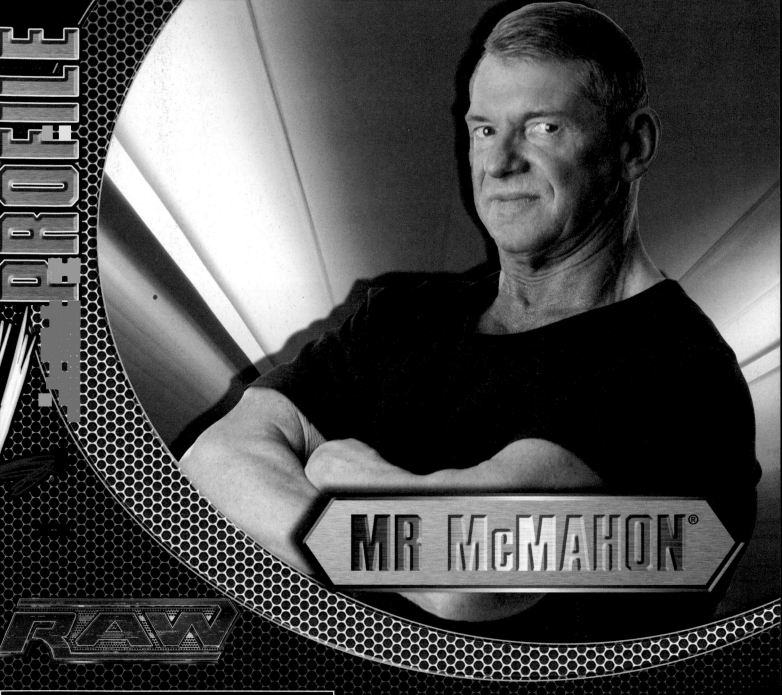

MR McMAHON

RAW

Height:	6-foot-2
Weight:	248 pounds
From:	Greenwich, CT
Career Highlights:	WWE Champion

Mr McMahon *WrestleMania* Record.

March 1985: Mr McMahon presented the first of many *WrestleMania's* on Closed Circuit TV.

March 1986: Mr McMahon went one step further and presented *WrestleMania II* on pay-per-view from three different venues.

March 1987: Mr McMahon promoted the largest event of his career at *WrestleMania III* with Hulk Hogan vs Andre The Giant.

WrestleMania 2000: Mr McMahon turned on The Rock, costing him the WWE Championship in the main event.

April 1, 2001 - *WrestleMania X-7:* Shane McMahon defeated Mr McMahon in a Street Fight.

March 30, 2003 - *WrestleMania XIX:* Hulk Hogan beat Mr McMahon in a Street Fight.

March 14, 2004 - *WrestleMania XX:* Mr McMahon gave a speech thanking fans on behalf of all WWE Superstars.

April 2, 2006 - *WrestleMania 22:* Shawn Michaels defeated Mr McMahon w/Shane McMahon in a No Holds Barred Match.

April 1, 2007 - *WrestleMania 23:* Bobby Lashley w/Donald Trump defeated Umaga w/Mr McMahon in a Hair vs Hair match, after which Mr McMahon got his head shaved bald!

March 28, 2010 – *WrestleMania XXVI:* Bret 'Hit Man' Hart defeated Mr McMahon in a No Holds Barred Match.

BRET HART®

Bret 'Hit Man' Hart has had a running war with WWE Chairman Mr McMahon ever since the Hall of Famer returned to *Raw*.

McMahon promised Hart a match at *WrestleMania XXVI* and then denied having done so. The boss man said he would have Stu Hart, Bret's father, inducted into the WWE Hall of Fame and then turned him down.

The simmering rivalry between Hart and McMahon needed sorting and what better way to settle the hostilities than a real grudge match! The prospect of a showdown between the pair at *WrestleMania XXVI* was something every WWE fan couldn't wait to see.

Bret Hart was on a mission to gain revenge and tricked McMahon

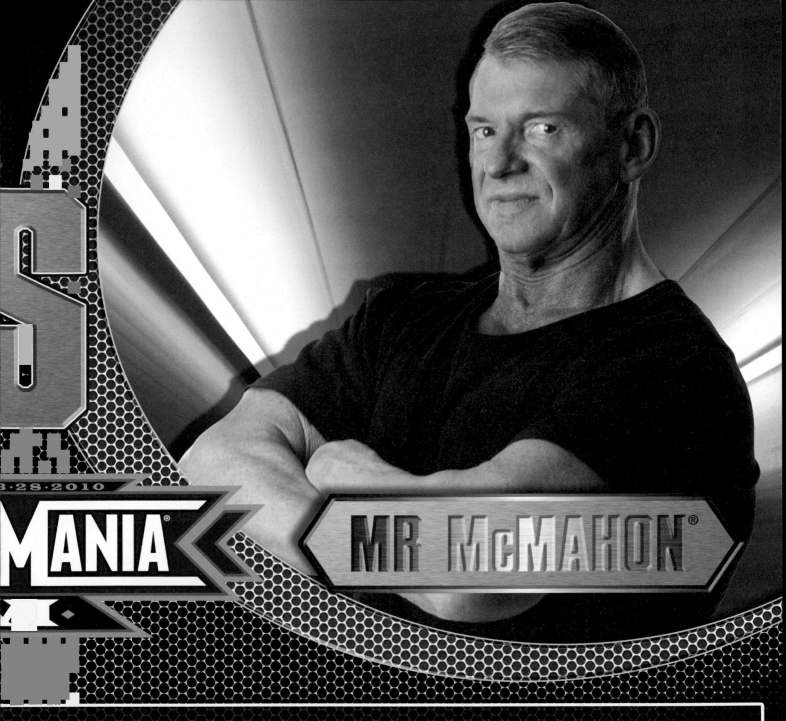

3·28·2010

MR McMAHON

into agreeing to a No Holds Barred Match between the pair at *WrestleMania XXVI*. Hart even faked a leg injury to fool McMahon into believing that he would be easy to beat.

Several surprise Lumberjacks surrounded the ring as the pair made ready for their historic clash- all members of the Hart family! McMahon had reputedly

paid the whole family to be on his side. Bret's brother Bruce was referee!

But little did McMahon realize that the tables were about to be turned on him big time. Little did he expect that he was about to suffer more than one crushing blow. Mr McMahon faced a much bigger task than he realized…

"And just listen to the reaction Bret Hart is getting from the WWE Universe!"

"Well this match has been thirteen years in the making, but here at *WrestleMania XXVI* it is finally going to happen!"

"Bret 'Hit Man' Hart has returned to WWE to face Mr McMahon!"

"Never has there been a more popular Superstar than 'The Hit Man'!"

"And never has there been a more hated figure in WWE than this man, WWE Chairman, Mr McMahon!"

"I don't believe it! Mr McMahon has paid off the entire Hart family. Look! There are all the Hart brothers and sisters along with The Hart Dynasty!"

"What does McMahon have planned here tonight?"

"McMahon has screwed Bret once again!"

"But wait! It's a case of the old switcheroo. The Hart family have taken the boss's money and turned on him!"

"This is not good for McMahon, he now has to face the entire Hart family in this match!"

"Bret has Mr McMahon down in the corner and is stomping away at the boss's face!"

"Thirteen years of hatred is being unleashed in that very ring tonight!"

"Mr McMahon is a billionaire owner of a multinational company. He should not be treated this way!"

"I don't think the rest of the WWE Universe would agree with that!"

"Mr McMahon is trying to escape up the aisle. David Hart Smith catches him with a huge right hand that leaves McMahon reeling!"

"The entire Hart family are assaulting Mr McMahon!"

"The boss needs to get out of here and quickly!"

"I think The Hart Dynasty can say goodbye to their WWE career after this match is over!"

"Did you see McMahon's head bounce off the concrete floor on the outside of the ring?"

"This match should be stopped. This is a gang beating!"

"What are Tyson Kidd and David Hart Smith thinking here? It couldn't be! A Hart Attack from the top rope to the outside!"

"Look at Tyson Kidd fly."

"I think our boss may have taken your advice, he is trying to crawl under the ring!"

"That's it Vince! Hide! There is no shame in it."

"McMahon is momentarily rolled back into the ring by some of the Hart sisters only to take another beating from Bret 'Hit Man' Hart."

"The Hart family have dragged the boss out from under the ring. And look, he has a tyre iron!"

"Run Mr McMahon. Just get out of there!"

"The Hart family aren't so tough now, are they? Go on Mr McMahon, show them who's boss!"

"But as soon as McMahon gets back into the ring, Bret easily takes the tyre iron off him and uses the weapon himself!"

"Well it is not just the Hart family that feel a strong dislike for Mr McMahon, it is the whole WWE Universe."

"Another brutal shot across the back!"

"Listen to the fans here tonight! They are actually encouraging this sickening display."

"And look at this! Bret is just taking a breather while Mr McMahon writhes around the ring in pain!"

"Could it be? Is Bret 'Hit Man' Hart about to apply the Sharpshooter?"

"Bret really wants to embarrass his former boss, just like McMahon did to him all those years ago!"

"No! Bret is not done with Mr McMahon yet. He wants to make him suffer even more!"

"Bret Hart with a huge chair shot!"

"That shot echoed around the arena!"

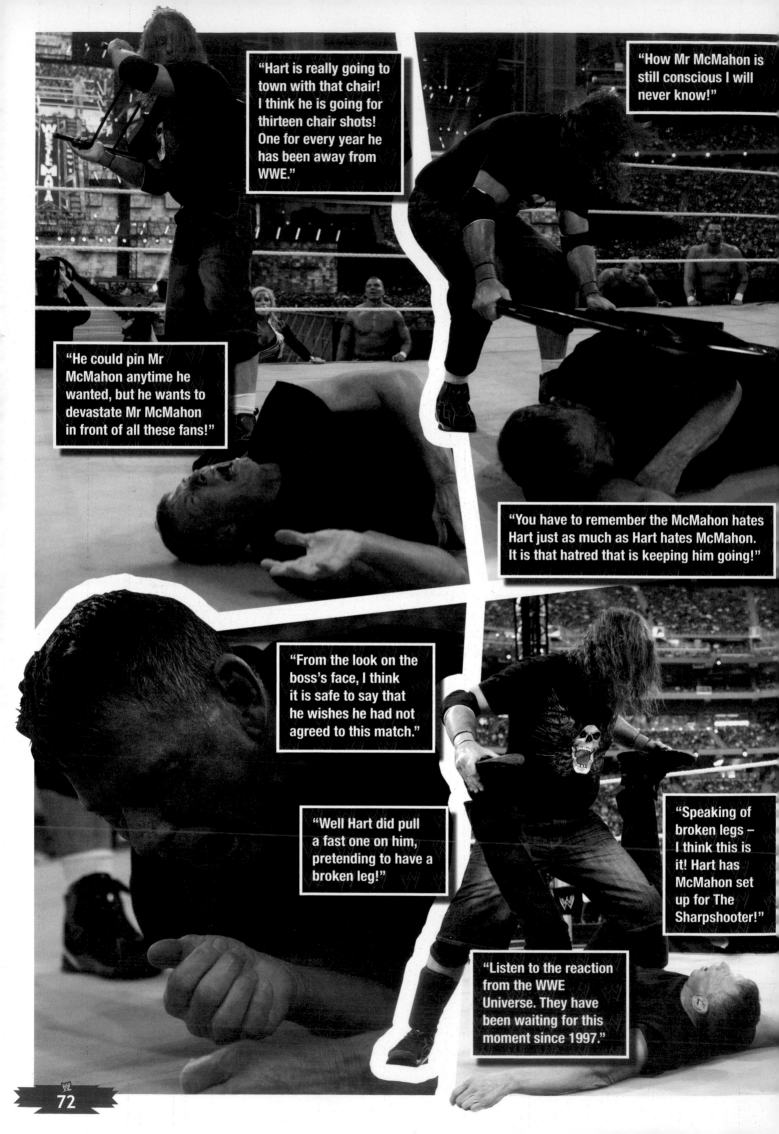

"Hart is really going to town with that chair! I think he is going for thirteen chair shots! One for every year he has been away from WWE."

"How Mr McMahon is still conscious I will never know!"

"He could pin Mr McMahon anytime he wanted, but he wants to devastate Mr McMahon in front of all these fans!"

"You have to remember the McMahon hates Hart just as much as Hart hates McMahon. It is that hatred that is keeping him going!"

"From the look on the boss's face, I think it is safe to say that he wishes he had not agreed to this match."

"Speaking of broken legs – I think this is it! Hart has McMahon set up for The Sharpshooter!"

"Well Hart did pull a fast one on him, pretending to have a broken leg!"

"Listen to the reaction from the WWE Universe. They have been waiting for this moment since 1997."

"Bret Hart has it locked in! Listen to the screams of agony from Mr McMahon. He will surely have to tap out!"

"And he does! But Bret is refusing to release the hold. Let him go Bret! Let him go!"

"Bret 'Hit Man' Hart has won the match and the crowd is going insane!"

"Bret 'Hit Man' Hart has returned to *WrestleMania* and has recorded perhaps the biggest victory of his career or at least one that means the most to him and his family!"

"It was not pretty or technical, but Hart did what he came here to do."

"Bret Hart has finally gained the closure he was looking for by defeating the boss in the middle of the ring!"

"And look at Mr McMahon. He is being helped to the back and he looks furious!"

"I don't think we have seen the last of this rivalry, not if McMahon has anything to do with it…"

COLOURING ACTIVITY

Check out the action from this year's Money in the Bank Ladder Match! Use your felt tip pens or pencils to add some colour!

SMACK DOWN

Name:	CM Punk
Height:	6-foot-1
Weight:	222 pounds
From:	Chicago, IL
Signature Move:	G.T.S. (Go to Sleep), Anaconda Vice
Career Highlights:	World Heavyweight Champion, ECW Champion

Name:	Rey Mysterio
Height:	5-foot-6
Weight:	175 pounds
From:	San Diego, CA
Signature Move:	619, West Coast Pop
Career Highlight:	World Heavyweight Champion

SMACK DOWN

Name:	Luke Gallows
Height:	6-foot-8
Weight:	302 pounds
From:	Cumberland, MD
Signature Move:	Twelve Steps
Associates:	CM Punk, Serena

Name:	Finlay
Height:	6-foot-2
Weight:	233 pounds
From:	Belfast, Northern Ireland
Signature Move:	The Celtic Cross
Career Highlights:	United States Champion

SMACK DOWN

Name:	Big Show
Height:	7-foot
Weight:	485 pounds
From:	Tampa, FL
Signature Move:	Chokeslam
Career Highlights:	WWE Champion, ECW Champion

Name:	Shad Gaspard
Height:	6-foot-7
Weight:	295 pounds
From:	Brooklyn, NY
Signature Move:	The Recoil
WWE Debut:	October 16, 2006

SMACK DOWN

Name:	Cody Rhodes
Height:	6-foot-1
Weight:	223 pounds
From:	Charlotte, NC
Signature Move:	Cross Rhodes
Career Highlight:	World Tag Team Champion

Name:	Caylen Croft
Height:	6-foot
Weight:	220 pounds
From:	Youngstown, Ohio
WWE Debut:	2009

Name:	Carlito
Height:	5-foot-10
Weight:	220 pounds
From:	San Juan, Puerto Rico
Signature Move:	Backstabber
Career Highlights:	Intercontinental Champion, United States Champion

Name:	Goldust
Height:	6-foot-6
Weight:	260 pounds
From:	Hollywood, CA
Signature Move:	Curtain Call, Golden Globes
Career Highlights:	Intercontinental Championship, World Tag Team Champion

Name:	Randy Orton
Height:	6-foot-4
Weight:	245 pounds
From:	St. Louis, MO
Signature Move:	RKO
Career Highlights:	WWE Champion, World Heavyweight Champion

Name:	Santino Marella
Height:	5-foot-10
Weight:	227 pounds
From:	Calabria, Italy
Signature Move:	The Cobra
Career Highlight:	Intercontinental Champion

Name:	John Morrison
Height:	6-foot-1
Weight:	223 pounds
From:	Los Angeles, CA
Signature Move:	Starship Pain, Moonlight Drive
Career Highlight:	ECW Champion

Name:	Mark Henry
Height:	6-foot-1
Weight:	392 pounds
From:	Silsbee, TX
Signature Move:	World's Strongest Slam
Career Highlight:	ECW Champion

Name:	The Miz
Height:	6-foot-1
Weight:	231 pounds
From:	Cleveland, OH
Signature Move:	Skull-Crushing Finale
Career Highlights:	United States Championship, Unified Tag Team Champion

Name:	William Regal
Height:	6-foot-2
Weight:	240 pounds
From:	Blackpool, England
Signature Move:	Regal Stretch
Career Highlights:	Intercontinental Champion, World Tag Team Champion

Divas

Name:	Alicia Fox
Height:	5-foot-9
From:	Ponte Vedra, FL
Career Highlight:	Wedding Planner for Edge and Vickie Guerrero

Name:	Brie Bella
Height:	5-foot-6
From:	Scottsdale, AZ
Career Highlight:	Manager to Carlito

Divas

Name:	Beth Phoenix
Height:	5-foot-7
From:	Buffalo, NY
Career Highlight:	Women's Champion

Name:	Kelly Kelly
Height:	5-foot-5
From:	Jacksonville, FL
Career Highlight:	In a music video for Timbaland "Throw It on Me"

Name:	Eve Torres	Name:	Gail Kim
Height:	5-foot-8	Height:	5-foot-4
From:	Los Angeles, CA	From:	Tampa, FL
Career Highlight:	Divas Champion	Career Highlight:	Women's Champion

Name:	Michelle McCool	Name:	Serena
Height:	5-foot-10	Height:	5-foot-4
From:	Palatka, FL	From:	Seattle, WA
Career Highlight:	First-ever Divas Champion, Women's Champion	Career Highlight:	First female member of CM Punk's Straight Edge Society

Name:	Daniel Bryan
Height:	5-foot-10
Weight:	190 pounds
From:	Aberdeen, WA
WWE Pro:	The Miz

Name:	Darren Young
Height:	6-foot-1
Weight:	240 pounds
From:	Miami, FL
WWE Pro:	CM Punk

Name:	David Otunga
Height:	6-foot
Weight:	240 pounds
From:	Hollywood, CA
WWE Pro:	R-Truth

Name:	Heath Slater
Height:	6-foot-2
Weight:	230 pounds
From:	Pineville, WV
WWE Pro:	Christian

Name:	Justin Gabriel		Name:	Michael Tarver
Height:	6-foot-1		Height:	6-foot-2
Weight:	215 pounds		Weight:	256 pounds
From:	Cape Town, South Africa		From:	Akron, OH
WWE Pro:	Matt Hardy		WWE Pro:	Carlito

Name:	Skip Sheffield		Name:	Wade Barrett
Height:	6-foot-2		Height:	6-foot-5
Weight:	270 pounds		Weight:	265 pounds
From:	College Station, TX		From:	Manchester, England
WWE Pro:	William Regal		WWE Pro:	Chris Jericho

UNDERTAKER®

THE Undertaker

SMACK DOWN

Height:	6-foot-10 1/2
Weight:	299 pounds
From:	Death Valley
Signature Move:	Chokeslam, Tombstone, Last Ride
Career Highlights:	WWE Champion, World Heavyweight Champion

Undertaker's *WrestleMania* Record.

March 24 1991 - *WrestleMania VII:* Undertaker w/Paul Bearer defeated Jimmy 'Superfly' Snuka.

April 5 1992 - *WrestleMania VIII:* Undertaker w/Paul Bearer defeated Jake 'The Snake' Roberts.

April 4 1993 - *WrestleMania IX:* Undertaker w/Paul Bearer defeated Giant Gonzales w/Harvey Wippleman by DQ.

April 2 1995 - *WrestleMania XI:* Undertaker w/Paul Bearer defeated King Kong Bundy w/Ted DiBiase.

March 31 1996 - *WrestleMania XII:* Undertaker w/Paul Bearer defeated 'Big Daddy Cool' Diesel.

March 23 1997 - WrestleMania 13: Undertaker defeated Sycho Sid to win the WWE Championship.

March 29 1998 - WrestleMania XIV: Undertaker defeated Kane w/Paul Bearer.

March 28 1999 - *WrestleMania XV:* Undertaker defeated Big Bossman in a Hell in a Cell Match.

April 1 2001 - *WrestleMania X-7:* Undertaker defeated Triple

March 17 2002 - *WrestleMania X8:* Undertaker defeated 'Nature Boy' Ric Flair.

March 30 2003 - *WrestleMania XIX:* Undertaker beat Big Show and A-Train in a Handicap Match.

March 14 2004 - *WrestleMania XX:* Undertaker w/Paul Bearer defeated Kane.

April 3 2005 - *WrestleMania 21:* Undertaker defeated Randy Orton in a Legend vs Legend Killer Match.

April 2 2006 - *WrestleMania 22:* Undertaker defeated Mark Henry in a Casket Match.

April 1 2007 - *WrestleMania 23:* Undertaker defeated Batista to capture the World Heavyweight Championship.

March 30 2008 - *WrestleMania XXIV:* Undertaker defeated Edge to capture the World Heavyweight Championship.

April 5 2009 - *WrestleMania XXV:* Undertaker defeated Shawn Michaels.

SHAWN MICHAELS

RAW

Height:	6-foot-1
Weight:	225 pounds
From:	San Antonio, TX
Signature Move:	Sweet Chin Music
Career Highlights:	WWE Champion, World Heavyweight Champion

Shawn Michaels' *WrestleMania* Record.

April 2, 1989 - *WrestleMania V:* The Twin Towers defeated The Rockers (Shawn Michaels & Marty Janetty).

April 1, 1990 - *WrestleMania VI:* The Orient Express defeated The Rockers.

March 24, 1991 - *WrestleMania VII:* The Rockers defeated Barbarian and Haku w/Bobby Heenan.

April 5, 1992 - *WrestleMania VIII:* Shawn Michaels w/ Sensational Sherri defeated 'El Matador' Tito Santana.

April 4, 1993 - *WrestleMania IX:* Tatanka defeated Shawn Michaels.

March 20, 1994 - *WrestleMania X:* Razor Ramon defeated Shawn Michaels in the first-ever Ladder Match.

April 2, 1995 - *WrestleMania XI:* Diesel defeated Shawn Michaels to retain the WWE Championship.

March 31, 1996 - *WrestleMania XII:* Shawn Michaels defeated Bret 'Hit Man' Hart in a 60-minute Iron Man Match.

March 23, 1997 - *WrestleMania 13:* Shawn Michaels joined commentary for the Undertaker vs Sycho Sid.

March 29, 1998 - *WrestleMania XIV:* Stone Cold Steve Austin defeated Shawn Michaels to win the WWE Championship.

March 28, 1999 - *WrestleMania XV:* Shawn Michaels made a surprise guest appearance before the main event.

March 30, 2003 - *WrestleMania XIX:* Shawn Michaels defeated Chris Jericho.

March 14, 2004 - *WrestleMania XX:* Chris Benoit beat Triple H and Shawn Michaels.

April 3, 2005 - *WrestleMania 21:* Kurt Angle defeated Shawn Michaels.

April 2, 2006 - *WrestleMania 22:* Shawn Michaels defeated Mr McMahon w/Shane McMahon.

April 1, 2007 - *WrestleMania 23:* John Cena defeated Shawn Michaels by Submission.

March 30, 2008 - *WrestleMania XXIV:* Shawn Michaels defeated 'Nature Boy' Ric Flair.

April 5, 2009 - *WrestleMania XXV:* Undertaker defeated Shawn Michaels.

UNDERTAKER®

It was set to be the ultimate battle: the undefeated champion against a Superstar seeking sweet revenge. At *WrestleMania 25*, the two top Superstars of WWE fought each other in their home state of Texas in what was later regarded as the match of the year.

The Showstopper and the Deadman stole the show then and a re-match was a mouth-watering

prospect. But at *WrestleMania XXVI* could Michaels end the Phenom's 17-0 winning streak? Or would Undertaker improve his record to 18-0?

Michaels challenged Undertaker to face him at *WrestleMania XXVI* on an episode of Raw but he was turned down. That meant Michaels had to win the *Royal Rumble* Match in order to get a title shot

MANIA

SHAWN MICHAELS

against the World Heavyweight Champion. But Michaels failed to win the *Royal Rumble* and was not on *SmackDown* and ineligible for the *Elimination Chamber Match* for Undertaker's World Heavyweight Championship.

Undertaker agreed to a rematch when Michaels cost him his World Heavyweight Championship when he interfered at *Elimination Chamber* 2010. But Michaels had to agree that he would retire if he lost the *WrestleMania XXVI* bout.

This was a clash with two massive reputations at stake and the chance that a distinguished 25 year old career could be brought to a sudden end.

"Can Undertaker pick him up though after the damage HBK caused to Undertaker's leg?"

"Undertaker has HBK caught by the throat! This does not look good for 'The Showstopper'."

"But Undertaker is too weak to make the cover. His knee may have given out on him there!"

"Undertaker takes him up and slams him down with a *WrestleMania*-sized chokeslam!"

"HBK has time to recover and goes back on the attack with an ankle lock!"

"Undertaker breaks the hold and rolls to the outside. HBK may be looking to fly here!"

"This is very wise from Shawn Michaels. Keep Undertaker on his back and you eliminate most of his offence."

"Oh good Lord no! Undertaker caught HBK in mid air and has him set up for a Tombstone Piledriver on the concrete floor!"

"HBK's head just bounced off the concrete. But Undertaker cannot win the match on the outside, he needs to get HBK back inside the ring."

"HBK sails over the top rope with a suicide dive on to Undertaker."

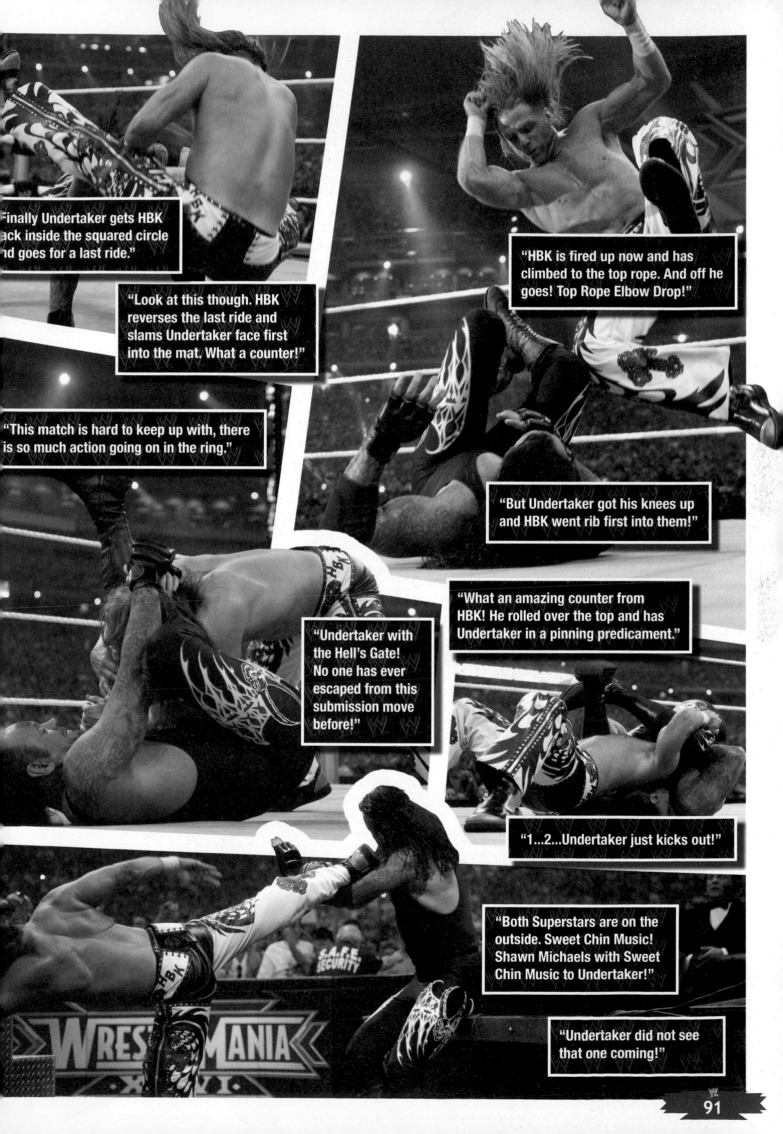

"Finally Undertaker gets HBK back inside the squared circle and goes for a last ride."

"Look at this though. HBK reverses the last ride and slams Undertaker face first into the mat. What a counter!"

"This match is hard to keep up with, there is so much action going on in the ring."

"Undertaker with the Hell's Gate! No one has ever escaped from this submission move before!"

"HBK is fired up now and has climbed to the top rope. And off he goes! Top Rope Elbow Drop!"

"But Undertaker got his knees up and HBK went rib first into them!"

"What an amazing counter from HBK! He rolled over the top and has Undertaker in a pinning predicament."

"1...2...Undertaker just kicks out!"

"Both Superstars are on the outside. Sweet Chin Music! Shawn Michaels with Sweet Chin Music to Undertaker!"

"Undertaker did not see that one coming!"

"Undertaker is laid out on our announce table. And HBK has climbed to the top of the corner post!"

"He is going to fly! Moonsault through the table! I have never seen a match like this before!"

"Shawn Michaels rolls Undertaker back into the ring and he is tuning up the band."

"A second Sweet Chin Music! Undertaker must be out! Make the pin Shawn!"

"Undertaker just sat right back up. Another chokeslam! This is amazing!"

"HBK's career may be over right here!"

"1...2...Undertaker again kicks out. Is it possible to beat 'The Phenom'?"

"Undertaker is not taking any chances now, he has HBK set up for yet another Tombstone!"

"If he hits it, the match is over, no doubt about it!"

"HBK kicked out after two! Shawn Michaels is clawing his way back to his feet! This match means so much to him."

"But I think he just asked Undertaker to finish it! I think he realises he is beaten!"

"Undertaker with a third Tombstone! Never before has a competitor survived this much punishment at the hands of Undertaker!"

"That's it! It must be over now!"

"Undertaker makes the pin! 1...2...3! Undertaker has won the match. Undertaker is still undefeated at *WrestleMania*!"

"And HBK's career is over! What an incredible battle!"

"A great show of respect from these two great competitors! Undertaker and Shawn Michaels showing what real sportsmanship is by shaking hands in the middle of the ring."

"They both gave it their all, but it is Undertaker who has come out on top."

"Goodbye Shawn Michaels and thank you for the memories."

"That is it from *WrestleMania XXVI*, thank you for joining us!"

WRESTLEMANIA

WELL DONE! YOU HAVE MADE IT TO THE MAIN EVENT SECTION OF THE *WRESTLEMANIA* QUIZ! HERE, ALL THE QUESTIONS ARE BASED AROUND THE TOP MATCHES AT PREVIOUS *WRESTLEMANIA* EVENTS SO YOU ARE REALLY GOING TO HAVE TO KNOW YOUR STUFF!

Q1 Who is this Superstar that competed in the main event at *WrestleMania X-Seven*?

A. Batista ☐
B. The Rock ☐
C. John Cena ☐

Q2 How many Superstars competed for the World Heavyweight Championship at *WrestleMania 22*?

A. 2 ☐
B. 3 ☐
C. 4 ☐

Q3 Who won the World Heavyweight Championship at *WrestleMania 21*?

A. John Cena ☐
B. Triple H ☐
C. Batista ☐

Q4 At which *WrestleMania* did John Cena face Shawn Michaels for the WWE Championship?

A. *WrestleMania 23* ☐
B. *WrestleMania XX* ☐
C. *WrestleMania XXIV* ☐

QUIZ PART FOUR

Q5 How many times has Undertaker appeared in the final match at *WrestleMania*?

A. 6 times
B. 3 times
C. 10 times

Q6 Who is this Superstar that was defeated by Undertaker at WrestleMania 13?

A. Diesel
B. Sycho Sid
C. Ahmed Johnson

Q7 At which *WrestleMania* was Shawn Michaels knocked out by Mike Tyson?

A. WrestleMania XIV
B. WrestleMania X
C. WrestleMania XV

Q8 Who won the first-ever Money In The Bank Ladder Match?

A. Edge
B. CM Punk
C. Rey Mysterio

Q9 Which is the only *WrestleMania* to have featured a Tag Team match as its Main Event?

A. The inaugural WrestleMania
B. WrestleMania II
C. WrestleMania III

Q10 Finally, which current WWE Superstar has competed in the most *WrestleMania* Main Events?

A. Triple H
B. John Cena
C. Randy Orton

HORRIBLE

Who? & Who?   Who? & Who?   Who? & Wh

96

HYBRIDS!

Have you ever wondered what the offspring of two WWE Superstars would look like! It's unlikely we will find out for real, but this is the next best thing. Can you tell which two Superstars have been put together in each of the images below?

| Who? & Who? | Who? & Who? |

Matt Striker can get a bit confused while doing commentary and has got all the *WrestleMania* Superstars' names mixed up! Can you help him out? He doesn't want to any dafter than he already is!

1. TAKEERRDUN

☐☐☐☐☐☐☐☐☐☐

2. LAMA CHEWS SHIN

☐☐☐☐☐ ☐☐☐☐☐☐☐

3. CAWS GAG JERK

☐☐☐☐ ☐☐☐☐☐☐☐

4. DIRTY CREWMEN

☐☐☐☐ ☐☐☐☐☐☐☐

5. I REVOKE RUG RICE

☐☐☐☐☐ ☐☐☐☐☐☐☐

ANAGRAMS!

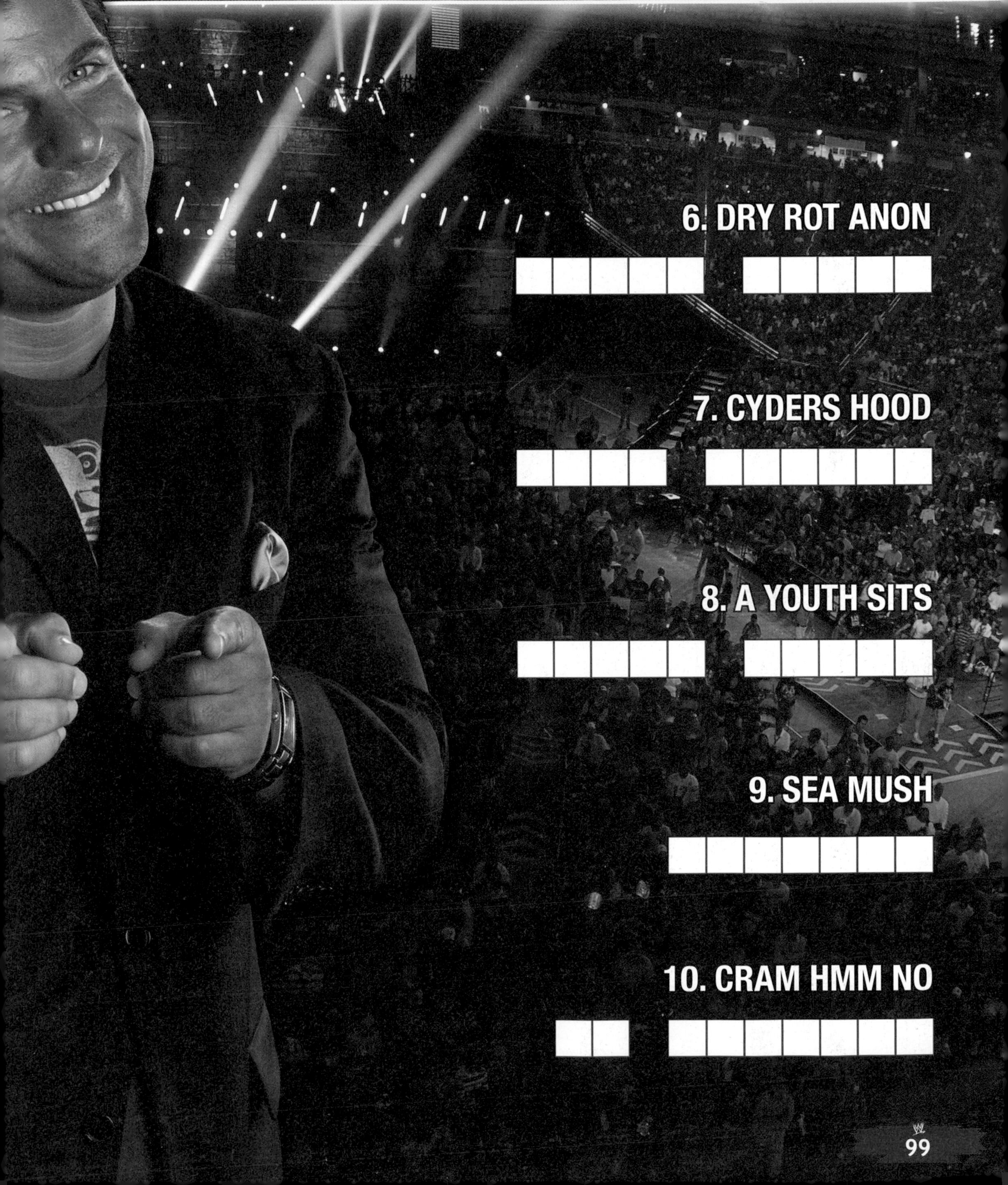

6. DRY ROT ANON

☐☐☐☐☐ ☐☐☐☐☐

7. CYDERS HOOD

☐☐☐☐ ☐☐☐☐☐☐

8. A YOUTH SITS

☐☐☐☐☐☐ ☐☐☐☐☐

9. SEA MUSH

☐☐☐☐☐☐☐

10. CRAM HMM NO

☐☐☐ ☐☐☐☐☐☐☐

MR McMAHON'S

Being the owner of WWE is no easy task. Not only does Mr McMahon have to deal with all the business side of things but, after a long day at the office, he then has guys like Bret 'Hit Man' Hart wanting to crack him with a steel chair! Can you help Mr McMahon find his way back to his office avoiding the Superstars who are out to get him?

FAREWELL TO HBK

H.B.K
Shawn Michaels

Whether you know him as The Heartbreak Kid, The Show Stopper, Mr *WrestleMania* or just plain old Shawn Michaels, you have to admit that his *WrestleMania* and WWE career has been the stuff of legend. Shawn Michaels made his *WrestleMania* debut alongside partner Marty Jannetty way back at *WrestleMania V* in 1989. Since then he has faced all-comers at the event and been a part of the greatest matches to take place in a WWE ring. At *WrestleMania XXVI*, all that came to an end when he was defeated by Undertaker and was forced to retire. Let's celebrate the career of HBK by taking a look at his last match, an instant classic! Use you felt tips or pencils to colour in these two pictures.

ARIZONA **W** 3·28·2010

WRESTLEMANIA
XXVI

/// RESULTS ///

UNDERTAKER DEF. SHAWN MICHAELS
IN A STREAK VS CAREER MATCH

BRET 'HIT MAN' HART DEF. MR McMAHON
IN A NO HOLDS BARRED MATCH

JOHN CENA DEF. BATISTA
NEW WWE CHAMPION

CHRIS JERICHO DEF. EDGE
WORLD HEAVYWEIGHT CHAMPIONSHIP

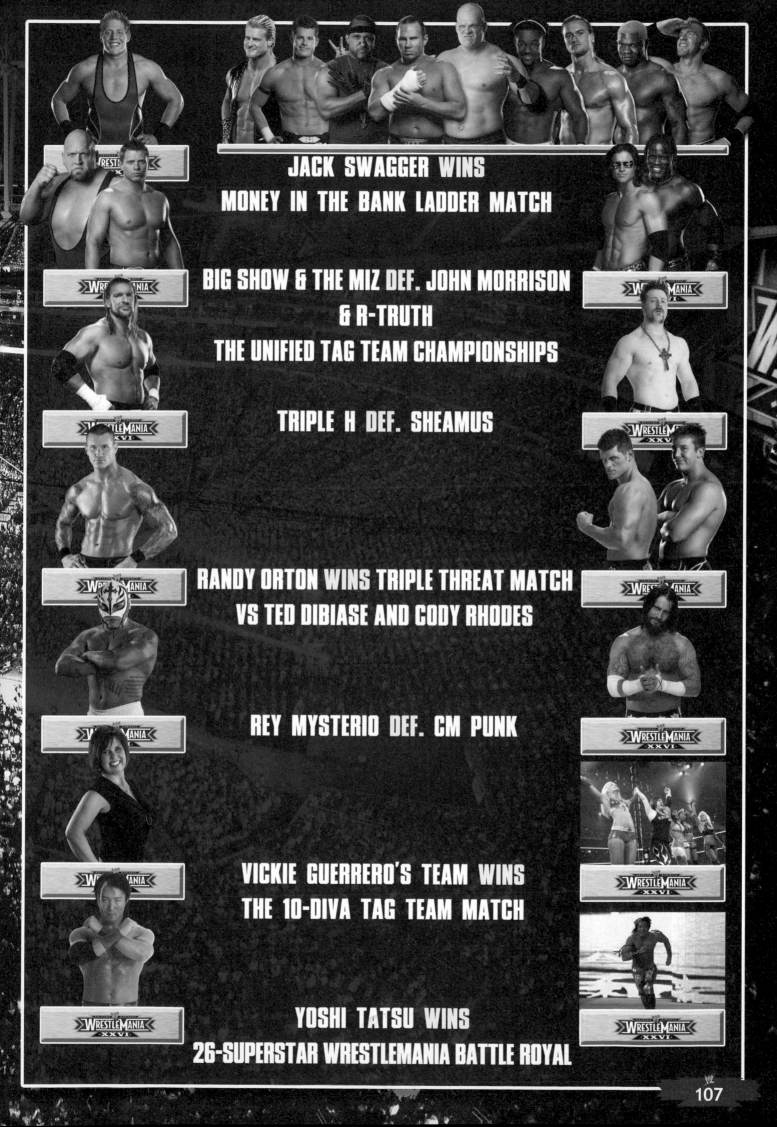

**JACK SWAGGER WINS
MONEY IN THE BANK LADDER MATCH**

**BIG SHOW & THE MIZ DEF. JOHN MORRISON
& R-TRUTH
THE UNIFIED TAG TEAM CHAMPIONSHIPS**

TRIPLE H DEF. SHEAMUS

**RANDY ORTON WINS TRIPLE THREAT MATCH
VS TED DIBIASE AND CODY RHODES**

REY MYSTERIO DEF. CM PUNK

**VICKIE GUERRERO'S TEAM WINS
THE 10-DIVA TAG TEAM MATCH**

**YOSHI TATSU WINS
26-SUPERSTAR WRESTLEMANIA BATTLE ROYAL**

ANSWERS

P18-19 *WrestleMania* Quiz Part One

1-A, 2-B, 3-A, 4-A, 5-A, 6-A, 7-C, 8-C, 9-B, 10-C.

P32-33 *WrestleMania* Quiz Part Two

1-C, 2-C, 3-B, 4-B, 5-C, 6-B, 7-A, 8-A, 9-B, 10-A

P34 *WrestleMania* Crossword

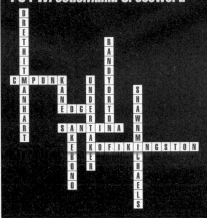

P34 *WrestleMania* Crossword

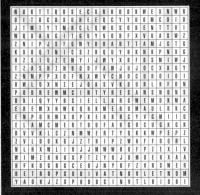

P46-47 Spot the Difference

P48-49 Hall of Fame Quiz

1-C, 2-A, 3-A, 4-B, 5-A, 6-C, 7-C, 8-B, 9-B, 10-C

P60-61 WrestleMania Quiz Part Three

1-Undertaker, 2-John Cena, 3-Finlay, 4-John Morrison, 5-Kofi Kingston, 6-Edge, 7-Big Show, 8-Rey Mysterio, 9-Matt Hardy, 10-William Regal

P94-95 WrestleMania Quiz Part Four

1-B, 2-B, 3-C, 4-A, 5-B, 6-B, 7-A, 8-A, 9-A, 10-A

P96-97 Horrible Hybrids

1-Edge & John Cena, 2-Kane & Santino
3-Triple H & Evan Bourne, 4-CM Punk & Rey Mysterio, 5-Big Show & Carlito

P98-99 Superstar Anagrams

1-Undertaker, 2-Shawn Michaels, 3-Jack Swagger, 4-Drew McIntyre, 5-Vickie Guerrero, 6-Randy Orton, 7-Cody Rhodes, 8-Yoshi Tatsu, 9-Sheamus, 10-Mr McMahon

P100 Mr McMahon's Maze

P104-105 The WrestleMania Locker Room.

Locker A - Bret 'Hit Man' Hart

Locker B - Undertaker

Locker C - Yoshi Tatsu

Locker D - Jack Swagger

Locker E - Drew McIntyre

Locker F - 'Million Dollar Man' Ted DiBiase